Running 101

Joe Henderson

Human Kinetics

Library of Congress Cataloging-in-Publication Data

Henderson, Joe, 1943-
    Running 101 / Joe Henderson.
    p. cm.
Includes index.
ISBN 0-7360-3056-5
    1. Running--Training. I. Title: Running one hundred one. II. Title: Running one hundred and
one. III. Title.

GV1061.5 .H46 2000
796.42--dc21   00-056690

ISBN: 0-7360-3056-5
Copyright 2000 by Joe Henderson

Acquisitions Editor: Martin Barnard; **Managing Editor/Graphic Artist:** Melinda Graham; **Assistant Editor:** John Wentworth; **Copyeditor:** Barbara Walsh; **Proofreader:** Pam Johnson; **Indexer:** Sharon Duffy; **Graphic Designer:** Nancy Rasmus; **Photo Manager:** Clark Brooks; **Cover Designer:** Jack W. Davis; **Photographer (cover):** ©Tony Demin/International Stock; **Printer:** United Graphics

Human Kinetics books are available at special discounts for bulk purchase. Special editions or book excerpts can also be created to specification. For details, contact the Special Sales Manager at Human Kinetics.

Printed in the United States of America   10 9 8 7 6 5 4 3 2 1

Human Kinetics
Web site: **http://www.humankinetics.com/**

United States: Human Kinetics, P.O. Box 5076, Champaign, IL 61825-5076
1-800-747-4457, e-mail: humank@hkusa.com

Canada: Human Kinetics, 475 Devonshire Road Unit 100, Windsor, ON N8Y 2L5
1-800-465-7301 (in Canada only), e-mail: humank@hkcanada.com

Europe: Human Kinetics, P.O. Box IW14, Leeds LS16 6TR, United Kingdom
+44 (0)113-278 1708, e-mail: humank@hkeurope.com

Australia: Human Kinetics, 57A Price Avenue, Lower Mitcham, South Australia 5062
(08) 82771555, e-mail: liahka@senet.com.au

New Zealand: Human Kinetics, P.O. Box 105-231, Auckland Central, 09-309-1890
e-mail: humank@hknewz.com

To Bert Nelson and Bob Anderson, the publishers
who put me on the running-writing course

Contents

Part I   Starting to Run

Part II   Running for Fitness

Part III Training to Race

Foreword

The year was 1960, in the Dark Ages before distance running became a popular participant sport. Ted Haydon, coach at the University of Chicago, had initiated a series of all-comers track meets for members of his team and other athletes looking for summer competition. One high school runner who showed up that year was Joe Henderson, visiting from Iowa.

That began our relationship that has lasted to this day. Joe would go on to win state cross-country and track championships, and I was a pretty good runner then too, finishing fifth in the Boston Marathon a few years later. Today we would be percieved as elite athletes, but then we were both beginners in the sense that we had only begun to learn about our chosen sport. Little had been published about how to train for long-distance races, and most of what did exist was wrong anyway.

Joe and I met again at the Olympic Games in Mexico City. By then he had joined the editorial staff of *Track & Field News*, a magazine that concerned itself more with reporting results than providing training tips. At the Games, I introduced Joe to Dr. George Sheehan, whose writing Joe would publish when he became editor of *Runner's World*. George would inspire many runners who were not elite. We all grew in our knowledge, and as we did, we passed that knowledge on to new runners attracted to our sport for its health benefits more than from a desire to win Olympic medals.

And here we are in a new millenium, continuing to preach to new runners, teaching them the basics of running, telling them how to run. *Running 101* is Joe Henderson's latest contribution to that effort. Turn these pages and enjoy learning about our sport. We're happy to have you join us.

Hal Higdon
Senior Writer, *Runner's World*

Acknowledgments

I learned to run by reading books. There was little choice, growing up in the rural Midwest where experts in distance running never ventured in person. My best lessons came by way of packages mailed from California-based *Track & Field News*, the only reliable source of running books at the time.

I'd never meet most of the teachers who came into my Iowa hometown this way and some I'd get to know only much later. I never thanked them for all that their words meant to me. In order read between the late 1950s and early '60s, they were: Franz Stampfl for *Stampfl on Running*; Percy Cerutty for *Running with Cerutty*; Arthur Newton for *Commonsense Athletics*; Fred Wilt for *How They Train*; and Arthur Lydiard for *Run to the Top*. If my latest book can have a fraction of the effect on you that these authors did on me, you'll make me a happy running writer.

What you read now isn't just my work but a team effort. The editorial team at Human Kinetics—Martin Barnard, Melinda Graham, John Wentworth, Nancy Rasmus, Barbara Walsh, Pam Johnson, and Sharon Duffy led me from this book's start line to finish line. I thank them for delivering *Running 101* to you in this package.

Photo Credits

Teaching and Learning

In my other life—which is to say, the one lived outside of the writing about running that has been my career since the 1960s—I moonlight as a university instructor. This involves teaching journalism classes at the University of Oregon, acting as the students' writing coach.

I started college myself with the plan of someday teaching in the classroom and coaching on the track. Life had other plans, though, detouring me into the family business of journalism (both parents worked in this field, as do two of my siblings and now a daughter of mine). Formal teaching didn't start for more than 20 years after graduation. Yet I've always been something of a teacher at heart, as well as in practice. I love to teach through articles, books, and talks. Nothing gives me greater pleasure than relaying advice to other runners.

I'm thrilled that Human Kinetics has given me a new chance to teach the fundamentals of this sport. Other books of this type feature the word "dummies" or "idiots" in their titles. We give more credit than that to your intelligence, experience, and seriousness of purpose. As our title suggests, this is a college-level course in running. You are the students, while I act as the professor. But the roles are blurred. I'm still learning after more than 40 years of running, racing, and writing. Many of the new lessons, or reminders of old ones, come from runners with less experience but clearer vision.

This book is not just for beginners. That term doesn't appear in the title because it would suggest that only new runners want to read this material or can learn anything from it. The basic lessons, rules, and practices of our sport apply to all. Only the details of application vary according to the experience, ability, and ambition of the runner. Runners everywhere ask me the same three questions:

1. How can I run farther (for instance, graduate from 10Ks or half marathons to marathons)?
2. How can I run faster (say, improve the 5K time by a minute or more)?
3. How can I get over my problems (injuries, both physical and emotional) from trying to run farther and faster?

This book doesn't stop at answering these three big questions. It covers (what else?) 101 topics, or lessons as they're labeled here. I address them as clearly and accurately as four decades of experience at learning and teaching allow. You might be learning these lessons for the first time, or relearning them after your own running has gone off course. Or you might use *Running 101* as a textbook if someone asks you that most flattering of questions: Will you teach me how to run better?

Lesson Index

PART I
Starting to Run

The umbrella of running has never cast a wider circle. Old runners, slow runners, heavy runners, and especially female runners have never felt more welcome. Whatever type of runner you are or want to become, you can find a home for yourself in this activity.

Chapter 1

Setting Goals

Find the approach that fits you best—from
basic training to long-distance racing.

The act of running is almost as straightforward as putting one foot
in front of the other and remembering to alternate feet. You don't
need a book to tell you how to do this. You started learning it when
you first toddled into a parent's outstretched arms and perfected
the act within the next year.

Lesson 1: Goals Overview

Running, the activity that transcends basic locomotion, isn't so
simple to introduce. One complication is that it's not a single activity but rather a collection of many activities huddled under one
umbrella. You can run for conditioning or competition, relaxation
or recreation, conversation or contemplation—or for two or more of
these reasons in combination. You can run short distances or long,
slow paces or fast—or some of each. You can specialize in running
or fit it into a wider-reaching fitness scheme that includes supplementary and complementary sports and exercises. You can be an
everyday, year-round runner or a part-timer who skips some days
or whole seasons.

   The umbrella of running has never cast a wider circle. The total
number of runners stands at an all-time high, and the scope of the

sport spreads ever outward. Old runners, slow runners, heavy runners, and especially female runners have never felt more welcome. Whatever type of runner you are or want to become, you can find a home for yourself in this activity.

First you need to identify your goal. Where do you want to go as a runner, and how can you best get there? You've already picked up a book to help you make those plans. After you've chased one goal for a while and finally achieved it, come back and aim for one of the many alternate goals.

Lesson 2: Running's Booms

Runner's World has labeled it the "second running boom." This isn't just a ploy to boost the magazine's circulation, which reached an all-time high as the 1990s ended. The second boomers fueled the increase. Let's talk about that boom so you can recognize your place in it.

Back in the 1970s we experienced a sudden 10-fold increase in the number of runners and running races. Most of the runners at that time were young men, and most of them took their racing quite seriously. This type of runner never went away, of course. The young and fast men will always be with us, but their percentage of the running population is shrinking.

The total population of runners has never shrunk since the first boom. It didn't end with a "bust" in the 1980s. The growth simply leveled off. Then the sport began to grow again in the 1990s, but in different ways than before. Running today is

• **bigger**. At the peak of the first boom, the number of marathon entrants in the United States never topped 100,000. Now, more than four times that many runners participate in marathons.

• **shorter** *and* **longer**. The most popular distance of the first boom was 10 kilometers. In fact, the majority of races were 10Ks. Now the most popular racing distances are 5Ks (with women's and corporate events contributing heavily to that growth) and marathons.

• **slower**. In the first boom the typical midpack time for a 10K was 40 to 45 minutes and for the marathon, 3:00 to 3:30. In the second boom we've added 10 minutes to the median 10K time and one hour to the marathon.

Taking the first steps to become a runner might lead to a lifelong love of running.

- **older.** Most of the runners from the first boom are still running in the second, and they naturally have aged by 20-plus years. They're joined by newcomers who discovered the sport in their middle age. The largest age groups at races are now late 30s and early 40s. (The exception to this aging trend is women in their 20s. This is the fastest-growing segment of women, who overall are the fastest-growing group of runners—now numbering 50 percent at many races.)

- **friendlier.** This isn't to say that the runners of the first boom were antisocial, but they tended to be loners. Second-boom runners are more likely to join a club, train with a coach in an organized program, run a race with a company team, or enter an event that raises money for charity. Runners today also treat races more as social events and vacations and less as the serious athletic contests that they once were.

Only the quality and depth of performances by leading Americans are now depressed. By all other standards—total number of runners, variety of runners (in terms of ability, age, size, and sex), events for runners, and resources available to runners—this is the best time ever to be a runner in the United States.

Lesson 3: Career Options

Running isn't a one-approach-fits-all-and-always activity. A runner can choose among many different approaches and can move from one to another as interests evolve. Typically a runner evolves through three stages: first as exerciser, then as racer, and finally as lifer.

None of these terms is precise, and the lines dividing them aren't clearly drawn. For simplicity's sake, though, we can say that an exerciser works out for fitness, a racer trains for competition, and a lifer runs purely to run. The first concern, then, is to become fit, then to push distances and paces to their limits, and finally to treat running as an end in itself.

In stage 1 you run mainly to regain and then maintain fitness. In stage 2 you're motivated to push your limits of distance and speed in company with other runners at organized events. In stage 3 you don't surrender fitness or necessarily leave racing behind. You can still race as well as many people who train just to race, and you can stay at least as fit as those who exercise only for fitness. But you don't *need* these results as much as you once did.

You don't leave the two earlier stages behind as you evolve into the third, but you simply modify them to fit your new view. You run more than the half hour, four days a week needed to maintain fitness, but less than the high-mileage weeks with long runs on weekends and speedwork in midweek needed to set records. The promise of a leaner body and stronger heart, or faster racing times or longer distances, become nice by-products of running instead of the main reasons that you do it.

Look now at what three prominent doctors say about these three stages.

Lesson 4: Fitness Running

Kenneth Cooper, MD, whose aerobics books are generally credited with putting America on the road to aerobic fitness, is not a fanatical runner. Though he ran competitively in high school and college and has exercised his way through the years since, he claims he doesn't even particularly like to run. However, he loves the results it gives him for a limited investment of time. Cooper's typical run lasts about 20 minutes, and he has mountains of data to prove this is enough to maintain fitness.

Fitness isn't the same as health. Health is a passive condition—the absence of disease or disability. Fitness is active—a learned capacity to work smoothly, efficiently, and with energy to spare. You can't sit and wait for fitness to come. You have to chase it by prodding, challenging, and stretching yourself. "You have to keep running," Lewis Carroll wrote in *Alice in Wonderland*, "just to stay where you are." To make further gains, you must run even more.

But how much more? Dr. Cooper's prescription for optimal running is two to three miles (3–5 kilometers), three to five days a week. "Anyone who runs more than 15 miles [25 kilometers] a week," he says, "is doing it for reasons other than fitness."

There are compelling reasons to run beyond the Cooper limit—training for races and running for recreation or relaxation, to name two. But realize that the extra running might add little or nothing to basic fitness and might even work against it by increasing the odds of injury. If all you want from running is a quick physical tune-up, simply follow the Cooper formula. Run modest distances at moderate efforts at least every other day.

Lesson 5: Sport Running

Joan Ullyot, MD, wrote the best-selling book *Women's Running* in the mid-1970s. But before she could write it, she had to live out the lessons she would pass on to other women.

Ullyot never ran until she was 30. She began for the usual reasons, to lose weight and to rid herself of the lingering effects of a smoking habit. A few years after struggling to complete a single lap on a running track, she improved enough to compete in the world marathon

As you start out in your running career, remember to build up slowly. Results won't come overnight, but they will happen with time.

championships. She continued to improve her race times into her 40s as she remained one of the top competitors in her age group.

Trained as a pathologist, Ullyot switched her specialty to exercise physiology after she became a runner. She carefully monitored the effects of training and racing, both on herself and on her patients, as she and they performed the tightrope act of running enough to improve but not so much that they broke down. The doctor devised a set of guidelines to manage these stresses. She called them the "Rules of 10":

1. "Increase the running by no more than 10 percent per week." A runner at a 25-mile (40-kilometer) weekly level, for instance, would step up to no more than 27-1/2 miles (44 kilometers).

2. "No more than one mile in 10 as speedwork." Our 25-mile-a-week (40-kilometer) runner would average no more than 2-1/2 miles (or 4 kilometers) of high-speed running, taken as either training or a race.

3. "You won't reach your full potential as an athlete until you have trained at least 10 years." This is true regardless of the runner's starting age. Witness Joan Ullyot herself, whose best marathon came in her 18th year of running. However, most runners notice their times leveling off after about a decade. The hard work provides fewer and lesser payoffs. That's when they start looking to downshift their intensity.

Running Commentary: Ten-Year Tenure

Joan Ullyot first told me about the 10-year rule. It might have originated with her—a medical doctor, a pioneering woman runner, and the author of *Women's Running.* "No matter what your age when you start running," said Joan, "you can expect about 10 years of improvement. That's how long it takes to learn the game."

This is true, she added, whether you start at 15 or 35 or 55. The 10-year clock clicks on whenever you start to run. Some runners cheat it, but usually not by much.

Through her knowledge gained from her years in medicine, plus a last big surge in her training, Joan herself stretched the timetable and achieved her PR (personal record) of 2:47 in her 12th year of marathoning, at age 48. The best-known beater of the 10-year rule was Carlos Lopes. He had raced for almost 20 years when he won the Olympic marathon and shortly thereafter set a world record. But injuries had forced his clock to stop for many years during that period.

For every Ullyot and Lopes who exceed the 10-year improvement norm, others fall short of it to correct the average. Jack Foster and Priscilla Welch both began racing in their mid-30s, and both set long-standing world masters marathon records seven to eight years later.

All of this warns you that your years of running fast times are limited. As an average figure, 10 years seems to work well. I like quoting this rule of thumb because it fit me perfectly. Long before I knew Joan Ullyot or realized that improvement wasn't indefinite, I ran out of room to run faster. I'd started racing shortly before my 15th birthday. My last PR of note came at 25.

Once the improvement warranty expires, then what—quit? Some runners do, but not many. Climbing to a peak in this sport doesn't mean that after arriving at the top of our game, we suddenly fall off a cliff. More likely there's a high plateau up there where many runners camp for a long time before starting a gradual decline. Others set off immediately to climb new and different peaks after reaching the first one. This has been my choice several times.

My first decade of running, from age 15 to 25, held the fast years. Permanent PRs came during this period in races as brief as 100 yards and 100 meters and as lengthy as the marathon (with the first and fastest coming in the last year of that cycle).

The second 10 years—from age 25 to 35—were my long years. More than half of my lifetime marathons, and all of my ultra attempts, fell into these years—as did my most career-threatening injury.

The next decade—35 to 45—held my lean years. Family and job complications sent me into semiretirement—where races were few and generally slow, and runs were regular but mainly short.

Running and racing revived in my fourth decade in the sport. These have been the mixed years of balancing long runs (marathons again after a long lull), fast runs (races as short as a mile), and easy days (often taken as voluntary rests, which I'd resisted in all earlier cycles).

My fifth decade of running has begun. It's too early to know what changes might come in this latest cycle, but I'm eager as ever to find out.

Lesson 6: Life Running

George Sheehan, MD, running's all-time favorite writer, once noted that "fitness is a stage you pass through on the way to becoming a runner." We might add that racing is a stage we pass through on the way to becoming a life runner.

Sheehan supplied a most eloquent description of lifers: "For every runner who tours the world running marathons, there are thousands who run to hear the leaves and listen to the rain, and look to the day when it is suddenly as easy as a bird in flight. For them, sport is not a test but a therapy, not a trial but a reward, not a question but an answer."

Derek Clayton once looked like the worst possible candidate to fit this definition. The Australian toured the marathoning world of the 1960s and early '70s, running this distance faster than anyone before him. He also trained harder than any marathoner ever had, and maybe that's why he reigned as the world-record holder for more than 12 years.

When he trained to a peak, Clayton ran up to 200 miles (320 kilometers) a week. The reward was his record, but there was also a toll to pay. His price was nine surgeries. On retiring from competition, Clayton made this blunt and revealing statement: "I can honestly admit now that I've never enjoyed a single minute of my running, and I'm relieved to be finished with it."

But his story didn't end there. Clayton's racing-induced injuries healed with time. He began to miss running a few months after he had retired. He didn't miss the 200-mile weeks and the marathons that had beaten him down so badly. He missed something about the daily routine of running itself.

Clayton began to run again. Only this time he limited himself to a half hour or so a day at a pace that was comfortable to him. He said his outlook on running changed from being grinding work that he barely tolerated to being "one of the bright spots in my day."

Running was no longer his test but his therapy, not his trial but his reward, not his question but his answer. You too can run like the man who once held a world record.

Lesson 7: Mile Test

Whatever your level of running involvement—exerciser, racer, or life runner—one of the best measures of your fitness is how well you run a measured distance for time. And the best-known distance for U.S. runners is one mile (1.6 kilometers). The time standards in Table 1.1 were developed for the *Runner's World* National Fun-Run Program, based on the 12-minute test of fitness icon Kenneth Cooper.

Test yourself with these directions: After a warm-up, run four laps on a standard 440-yard or 400-meter track, or a carefully measured mile on a flat course. Don't race at full speed, but run at a comfortable pace, taking walk breaks if necessary. Place yourself in one of the three levels of fitness—high, average, or low—according to your time, sex, and age. Note that time standards don't compare you to top-level athletes but rate your fitness against that of the general population.

Table 1.1 Mile Trial

Age group	High fitness	Average fitness	Low fitness
Women			
13–19	sub-7:00	7:00 to 8:29	8:30-plus
20–29	sub-7:30	7:30 to 8:59	9:00-plus
30–39	sub-8:00	8:00 to 9:29	9:30-plus
40–49	sub-8:30	8:30 to 9:59	10:00-plus
50–59	sub-9:00	9:00 to 10:29	10:30-plus
60–plus	sub-9:30	9:30 to 10:59	11:00-plus
Men			
13–19	sub-6:00	6:00 to 7:29	7:30-plus
20–29	sub-6:30	6:30 to 7:59	8:00-plus
30–39	sub-7:00	7:00 to 8:29	8:30-plus
40–49	sub-7:30	7:30 to 8:59	9:00-plus
50–59	sub-8:00	8:00 to 9:29	9:30-plus
60–plus	sub-8:30	8:30 to 9:59	10:00-plus

Lesson 8: Record Keeping

You can be your own biographer. You don't need to be a talented writer to profit from a diary. You don't need to spend more than a minute a day writing in it. You don't even have to write many, or indeed any, words. Numbers alone tell stories as they recall old training sessions and suggest new possibilities. That process begins with three guidelines:

1. **Keep it simple**. Limit the amount of information to a few essentials that can be listed briefly, quickly, and in an accessible form for review. The harder it is to keep a diary, the less likely you are to use it. You don't need a preprinted training diary. A calendar with large blocks of space for each day will do nicely as long as it is tacked to your bedroom or office wall, but it won't travel or store well. A notebook works best for this purpose. Fill it at the rate of one, two, or a few lines a day.

2. **Keep it up**. Analyze the accumulating data over extended periods to judge your results. Review at the end of each week, month, and year. The longer you maintain the diary, the clearer your patterns become of response to the exercise—and the clearer your thinking about it. Days of training leave behind what appear to be random footsteps in the diary. You can't take much direction from them at first. But the weeks, months, and years form a trail that points in two directions. It shows where you have been and where you might go next.

3. **Keep it**. Store your records in a safe place, treating them as the precious volumes they will become in time. Their value grows along with their age and bulk. The ultimate value of a diary is as a personal library of dreams and memories. You can open it to any old page and bring a day back to life. You can call up a mental videotape and, from a few statistics on the page, re-create all you did and felt that day. These recordings give substance and permanence to efforts that otherwise would be as temporary as the moment and to experiences that would be as invisible as footprints on the pavement.

Chapter 2

Choosing Gear

Dress for safety, comfort, and performance in
shoes and clothing designed for you.

Lesson 9: Equipment Overview

Running is a minimalist activity, and the cost of getting in motion
needn't be high. You can equip yourself with the basics for less than
you'd spend on a movie and dinner for two. All you really need is a
good pair of shoes to keep the surface from biting you, and the minimal clothing required for modesty and comfort. The runner's requirements are few, but the choices are many.

Take shoes, for instance. One pair might last half a year or more
and cost less than a dime per mile of wear. But few runners settle for
a single pair. We rotate several models for special purposes—training and racing, roads and all-terrain. And we jump from model to
model, brand to brand in search of the elusive perfect shoe.

As runners, we could make our clothing selection as simple as
pulling any old grubbies from closets and drawers. But we want
more. The shirts and jackets, shorts and pants must feel just right.
Fabrics must breathe and wick but must not restrict movement or
tear flesh. And comfort aside, we dress not just for function but also
for fashion. Styles keep changing, so we make new purchases even
before our old clothes wear out.

Accessories also abound—inserts for shoes, supports for knees,
packs for supplies, shades for eyes. The most helpful—you might

say vital—accessory goes on your wrist. This can be a cheap digital stopwatch for checking your running times, a higher-tech device that records splits for later recall, or even an onboard computer that directs effort by measuring heart rate.

The marketplace has upped the sophistication, and the prices, of runners' wants. But our true needs remain few and fairly inexpensive.

Lesson 10: Choosing Shoes

First, consider your shoe needs. Chances are you are running modest distances at gentle paces, not double-figure amounts each day at Olympian speed. Possibly you're heavier than you'd like to be, and you aren't fully conditioned to tolerate the pounding inflicted by hard surfaces.

If any part of this description fits you, look for well-cushioned, well-supported shoes with the following features: a soft, nonirritating upper material (mostly nylon rather than leather), adequate toe room (a function of size and the cut of the shoe); a combination of sole materials (durable on the outside with a softer midsole for comfort), a heel lift (a wedge that raises the heel higher than the sole), heel protection (in the form of a rigid "counter" around the back for stability), and forefoot flexibility (so the foot can bend easily).

Many well-established manufacturers stand ready to fill these needs. A dozen leading brands are, alphabetically: Adidas, Asics, Brooks, Converse, Etonic, Fila, Mizuno, New Balance, Nike, Puma, Reebok, and Saucony. Choose shoes from any of these companies, whose models are discussed regularly in running-magazine surveys, and you can trust their quality.

Prices vary enormously. You can pick up little-known knockoff brands in discount stores or from mail-order houses for less than $30 U.S., and you can splurge on high-tech models that cost around $150. Avoid both extremes. You can protect yourself quite well with name-brand shoes averaging $75. For advice on selection and fit, ask a salesperson in a running specialty store or an experienced runner.

Another consideration is your foot type. Doctors specializing in foot health generally categorize feet in two ways, either floppy or rigid. The floppy foot tends to be flat and needs greater firmness and stability from shoes, whereas the rigid foot shows extremely high arches and requires more cushioning and flexibility.

The first step in avoiding shoe-related injury is choosing the right shoe. The second step is not letting your shoes grow too old. All shoes break down from hard use, losing cushioning and support. The critical factor is excessive wear at the heels. Most runners grind down their heels slightly to the outside of center. This gradually tips the foot plant out of balance.

When the hard outer layer of sole—usually about a quarter inch (or half a centimeter) thick—is worn through, the extra stress on the feet can become troublesome. When shoes reach this condition, re-tire and replace them. Five hundred miles (800 kilometers) of running is as much useful service as you can expect from your shoes.

You can extend this life span by not wearing the same pair of shoes for each run. Buy two or more pairs and alternate them. This has the same effect as rotating tires on a car. Each shoe brand and model—and even the same shoe at various stages of wear—creates different stresses on the feet and legs. Balance out these stresses by not wearing the same pair too many days in a row.

Running Commentary: Shoe Safety

A story out of Canada received lots of ink and airplay on both sides of the border. I first heard it on National Public Radio, then received a *Toronto Globe and Mail* story from a Canadian friend of mine, John McGee. The newspaper article's provocative headline: "Pricey Shoes Overrated, Report Says." Its subhead read, "Cheap footwear offers just as much protection to runners as the expensive kind."

Reporter Beverly Smith's story began, "People are being duped by claims that expensive athletic footwear is safer than cheap shoes, according to a Canadian report published in the *British Journal of Sports Medicine*. Advertising claims of superior cushioning and protection create a false sense of security in the user and actually increase the chance of injury." These were the findings of a study by Steven Robbins and Edward Waked of McGill University in Montreal.

Reading only a newspaper summary of research is risky, because reporters tend to oversimplify (or even misconstrue) certain aspects of scientific reports and to sensationalize others. John McGee, a running columnist for an Edmonton newspaper, wanted my views on the subject. My response: It's as misleading to say that shoes "cause injuries" as to claim that they "prevent injuries." In both cases the shoes are probably minor players. The main cause of injuries has always been, probably still is, and may always be mistakes in the way we run. Meaning: too much, too fast, too often.

That said, I can tell you that the percentage of runners getting hurt has dropped steadily since the 1970s. Back then *Runner's World* surveys indicated that about two-thirds of runners experienced injury within any year (an injury being defined as anything serious enough to disrupt the routine). The figure has since dropped to about 50 percent of runners injured per year, which is still too high.

Credit for our improving safety flows in two directions: (1) Runners have grown smarter, or at least more conservative, in their training over the years; and (2) manufacturers have improved the protective qualities of shoes. The real answer is probably some of both, but my guess is the first factor is the more important of the two.

I've known about the studies and conclusions of Steven Robbins (the main author of the McGill study) since the 1980s. His long-standing thesis is that the best shoe is the least shoe, and that we might be best off running barefoot.

I too happen to prefer the least of all shoes. But while Robbins uses science to support his contention, mine is just a personal preference and not a claim that anything is wrong with the way most of today's shoes are made or marketed. My unscientific bias is that choosing shoes is less a matter of safety (or even performance) than of comfort. I'm most comfortable in light, flimsy shoes. This is out of step with the majority of today's runners, who feel best in more substantial models.

To each his or her own. I don't think other runners are suffering for their choices, and neither am I.

Lesson 11: Softening Surfaces

A popular myth about running says that pounding along on hard surfaces is more likely to produce injuries, whereas soft surfaces such as grass and dirt are kindest to the feet and legs. But a *Runner's World* survey of thousands of runners indicated that grass and dirt runners got hurt just as often as those who ran entirely on asphalt or concrete. The study concluded that errors in the running routine are more likely to cause problems than the running surface.

Improvements in shoes have neutralized much of the pounding experienced on hard surfaces, creating portable soft surfaces, and most runners now use roads, for several reasons. Streets generally are well-lighted for running at any hour; they are runnable in all weather conditions; and they offer sure, smooth footing.

Running on smooth pavement can be easier on your body than running on softer surfaces.

Illogical as it might appear, these surfaces might be the best place to run if you're coming off an injury. Though you might think staying off roads would protect an injury, the feet and legs often respond better to streets and roads than to grass and dirt. This isn't because the roads are hard, but because they are smooth. Rough ground causes twisting stresses that can aggravate pain in, say, the knee or the Achilles tendon.

Although practicalities dictate that much of your running will be on hard surfaces, don't deprive yourself completely of the softer ones. The statistics in the study mentioned earlier ignore one key fact. The minor aches (as opposed to true injuries) runners suffer from constant pounding are clearly greater on hard road surfaces, and the soft surfaces are more pleasing esthetically.

Going soft might require a new pair of shoes. Today's typically bulky, thick-soled, well-supported models are designed for road running. They work less well when the going is soft and uneven. Off-road, your better choice is a somewhat flimsy racing shoe. Its thinner sole and greater flexibility keep you in better balance by putting you in closer touch with the rough ground.

Lesson 12: Weather Wear

Gone are the days of baggy gray sweatsuits, cotton gym shorts, and unmarked undershirts as standard running gear. Weatherproof jackets and pants (can't call them "sweats" anymore), and sweat-wicking singlets and shorts, all made of synthetic fabrics, are all the rage. Runners who could once outfit themselves for racing for $25 U.S., counting the cost of shoes, might now spend 10 times that much.

It's not necessary to spend that kind of money. To be sure, some of the new items have made running more comfortable, but many of them are more fashionable than functional. You should concern yourself with function—with what effect your clothing has on performance.

What are the essentials? Good shoes and whatever else feels comfortable. Dress for comfort, conditions, protection, and concealment, not for show.

How do you know how much clothing is enough? Check the weather forecast and add or subtract items depending on how hot

A variety of clothing options makes running in any type of weather possible.

or cold the day is—or how wet. This advice might appear obvious, except that temperatures on the thermometer are not what they seem. Runners more often overdress than underdress because they think the temperature at the starting line will remain constant throughout the run or race. But it never does.

The human body works very effectively as a furnace but rather poorly as an air conditioner; it creates heat better than it dissipates that warmth. As a result, the air temperature feels warmer by about 20 degrees Fahrenheit (or about 11° Celsius) during a run. This means that a pleasant day soon feels steamy, but also that a near-freezing temperature soon feels pleasant.

Dress with that temperature rule in mind. Start out feeling a bit underdressed and chilly, knowing that later you'll be cozy while runners around you are sweating in or stripping off their fashionable, expensive clothes.

Clothing serves a similar purpose to shoes. Whereas the shoes neutralize the hard surface, clothing (or lack of it) helps control the harsh climate. Start from the basics of shoes, running shorts, and underwear, and add layers according to the conditions. Table 2.1 lists some guidelines to help you dress for different types of weather conditions.

Lesson 13: Abundant Accessories

What else do you need besides shoes? Not much, although lots of manufacturers want you to sample their products. A typical issue of a running magazine displays a fascinating array of accessories. While applauding the ingenuity of American business, you can treat most of these items as luxuries or curiosities. Few offer much direct benefit to your running, and some can actually detract from it. However, five classes of products might contribute significantly to your running health and pleasure:

• Digital watches (see Lesson 14, page 24). These have become as essential as shoes and shorts. The cheap and versatile stopwatches become a coach on your wrist, accurately timing each run. Recommended are watches that store multiple splits for post-run review, and those with alarms that signal intervals of running and walk breaks.

• Heart-rate monitors that objectively plot your effort. Pulse is a more reliable measure of effort than pace is. The monitor is especially valuable for runners who need an objective measure of when and how to run easier on their easy days and to start slower in races.

• Inserts for running shoes, ranging from shock-absorbing heel pads and arch supports to over-the-counter orthotics. These products typically give more protection than the insoles manufactured into the shoes.

Table 2.1   Climate Control

Perceived condition	Actual temperature	Clothing to wear
Hot	Above 70° F (Above 21° C)	Add only the skimpiest singlet (tank top) and shorts that modesty will allow; men may choose to go shirtless and women to wear only a sports bra. Remember that high humidity makes hot days feel even hotter.
Warm	50-69° F (10-20° C)	Add a short-sleeved T-shirt to the basic uniform.
Cool	30-49° F (0-9° C)	Add long pants or tights and a long-sleeved shirt or light jacket at near-freezing temperatures.
Cold	Below 29° F (Below 0° C)	Add a layer of protection for hands and ears and perhaps another layer for legs and face in extreme cold. Remember that high wind makes cold days feel even colder.
Rain	Warm	Add a cap with a bill to keep vision clear; otherwise dress as on any warm day.
Rain	Cool	Add a cap plus a water-repelling jacket and pants; don't wear cotton sweats, which soak up water.
Snow	Cold	Add extra socks to keep feet warm and dry; be sure the shoes provide adequate traction on slippery roads.

• Bottle belts for carrying water or other liquids. This allows you to drink when you want during long runs alone and ensures a water supply during crowded races when you can't fight your way to a drink table. The belts can also hold food, keys, and identification.

• Reflective vests or clothing for running at night. You're most invisible to drivers on dark streets unless you wear something that shows up in their headlights. Cars are the biggest and most prevalent danger a runner ever faces, and this is one easy way to lessen the risk of being hit.

Lesson 14: Taking Time

It's a simple question: "How far did you run today?" Runners ask it of each other, and nonrunners sometimes feign interest by asking about our distances. Most runners in the United States answer with a number of miles, and everywhere else in the world the accounting is usually done in kilometers.

A better question, though, might be, "How *long* did you run today?" A better answer would be stated in hours and minutes instead of miles or kilometers. Running by time periods instead of distances is a more accurate way of keeping score, and it's made easier by the ready availability of digital stopwatches.

George Sheehan liked to ask his audiences, "What do you think is the greatest advance since the running boom of the 1970s?" Opinions ranged from better training and more races to finer shoes and improved diets.

"Those are all good guesses," Sheehan would say. "But I think the greatest advance is right here," and he would pull back his blue sleeve (he always wore a blue sweater) and point to the watch on his wrist. "This has made possible the personal record," he'd say. The sport couldn't have grown as it did unless each of us had a way of telling we were winning.

Before digitals, self-timing was a guessing game. Watches with hands were hard to set precisely and had a bad habit of stopping from shock or gumming up with sweat. The new watches made possible the reliable recording of times in races, and runners continued the practice during everyday training. Some runners came to like the ease of timing so much that they ran strictly by time periods and ignored distance, the day's run going into the logbook simply as "30 minutes" or "1:00."

The convincing reasons for starting to run by time are practical ones. This is a way to keep records without having to measure a course and then follow it as calibrated. You can detour from the prescribed route and go exploring without messing up the final result. When you're traveling away from home, time remains a constant, however unfamiliar the route. You don't need to guess at how long the run was.

You continue to run by the watch for physical, psychological, and philosophical reasons. These have to do with easing down and making friends with time. When you're running by distance and wearing a watch, time becomes your enemy. You try to beat a deadline—your personal record for that training loop or your goal for that day. The natural urge when running a distance is to push harder and finish sooner. Every second beyond the deadline is a little defeat.

When you're running to fill a time quota, however, the reverse is true. You can't make that time pass any faster by rushing, so you settle into a pace that feels right to you at the moment—neither too fast nor too slow. Each minute beyond the quota is a little victory.

Despite these attractions, time runners are still in the minority. Waves of fresh converts are arriving, though, by way of the newly popular walking break. Walking by distance isn't practical and often isn't even possible. Say you want to run a mile or a kilometer and then walk 100 yards or 100 meters. Distance marking at races is spotty, and you'll never see another mark 100 yards or meters later. Plotting your training courses this way is too much work, especially since it's unnecessary. Easier by far is letting the watch do all the work, signaling the intervals and recording the total time.

Chapter 3
Making Plans

Design the framework of running—when and where you run, your form, and your friends.

Lesson 15: Planning Overview

Journalism 101 classes teach writers the basics of writing a news story. They're taught to ask the five Ws and the H: who, what, when, where, why, and how. Stories are built around these answers.

Running 101 asks you to address these same questions for yourself. The answers form the infrastructure of your program. You've already answered the why-you-run question, or you wouldn't be reading this book. Later chapters, those detailing specific training and programs, tell you what to run. This chapter deals with the remaining three Ws and the H.

When? Time is a key raw material in the making of a runner. You need to carve out some of it nearly every day for doing your training. Fortunately, running is time-efficient. Few runners need more than an hour a day, and most can make do on a half hour.

Where? Anyplace that is walkable is runnable, which means you have no shortage of running spots. But some are safer, more pleasant to look at, and easier on your legs than others. Plot a variety of courses that are kindest to the body and soul.

Who? Decide who you want to share your runs, if anyone. Do you prefer to run alone for contemplation, with a partner or small group for conversation, or with a crowd for competition? You can run with people or away from them, as you choose.

How? This is a question of form or style. How do you look when you run? Is your running relaxed and efficient, or do style flaws hold down your distance and pace? Some matters of form are inborn and best left alone. But you can reduce or erase other faults to take the brakes off your progress.

Lesson 16: When, Where?

The most common reason given for not running—or not running more—is, "I don't have any time. I'm too busy." No one has the time if he or she doesn't want to find it. If you want to run, you *make* the time and stick to it. Whether you run in the morning, at noon, or at night, the effects are about the same. When you run depends on your schedule and your "body time." If you awaken bright-eyed, get up a little earlier. Morning is the most practical time for running, because seldom do you have anything else to do at that hour except sleep. Traffic is light. The air is coolest and cleanest at dawn. Showering and dressing are already part of the morning routine.

Noontime running is ideal if you have a long lunch break and a nearby place to exercise and clean up. Noon gives the triple benefit of a run in the daylight, a change of pace from the workday or school day, and a chance to avoid eating a heavy lunch.

Evening runs are easiest to skip. You come home tired and hungry. Your mind rebels at the thought of running and postponing dinner, but once you get going you find it's a relaxing way to end the day.

The second most common excuse for not running is, "I don't have any place to run." Look around you. Anywhere you can walk, you can also run.

"Running country is everywhere," said coach Bill Bowerman. "Open your door, and you're in business. Run right out the door, run in a schoolyard, on a city street, at the beach, on a country road, or in a vacant lot. Run down a bicycle path, on a school track, around a golf course, through a park, in your backyard, in a gymnasium, in a supermarket parking lot. Anywhere."

You might not have what seems to be an ideal place to run, such as a path laid out specifically for running as in Bowerman's hometown of Eugene, Oregon. But there are always plenty of other places—the streets, if nowhere else.

To save time, find places to run that are near home, school, or work—the nearer the better. It's best if you can start and finish most runs at your front door. These routes can take several forms: out-and-back (meaning you retrace your steps on the way home), lap (repeated circuits), or loop (single large lap) courses. Point-to-point courses start in one place and finish in another.

Map out routes that avoid congested areas as much as possible and are pleasant to run through. If you're interested in timing yourself, measure the courses. Accuracy of measurement depends on the

Not everyone has access to beautiful beaches for running, but you can run just about anywhere.

method used. Race courses must meet exacting standards, and they are checked with measuring wheels and steel tapes. However, your daily needs aren't that critical. Simply drive your course in the car, realizing that this method almost always produces routes slightly shorter than you think they are.

Running Commentary: Identify Yourself

Her name was Victoria Place, but no one knew it at the accident scene or later at the hospital. She was running near her Des Moines, Iowa, home when a car struck her as she crossed a street.

The woman flipped into the air, landed on her head, and was hurt too badly to identify herself. She'd been running alone, and none of the runners who arrived after the accident knew her. She carried no identification.

Steve Bobenhouse, who owns the Fitness Sports store in Des Moines, said later, "The second tragedy of the situation was that relatives could not be notified for five hours. A picture of her from the scene of the accident had to be broadcast over the TV before she could be identified."

Meanwhile, doctors had treated her without knowing who she was or what her medical history or possible reactions to medication might have been. The story ended well, with Victoria surviving her injuries and leading runners in her community to rethink the common practice of training in complete anonymity.

"Too many people run without carrying identification with them," said Bobenhouse, whose store serves more runners than any other in his state. "I know that I did it for 20 years."

I plead guilty, too. My running extends back even longer than Steve's, and the only times I'd ever identified myself was when I wore a race number. I was lucky never to have needed more than that.

Not wanting to dwell on an incapacitating injury or illness occurring during a run, I did nothing to prepare for this possibility, remote as it might be. I nearly always ran only with my dog, unknown to anyone who might pass.

The dog carried an identifying tag, but I wore none. (Mingo disappeared without wearing his license tag last winter and spent several miserable days in the pound as a "John Dog" before we tracked him down.) Imagine having an official trying to track down my name, address, and phone number by calling Animal Control.

After promising Steve Bobenhouse I would mend my ways, I began running with a simple—and possibly inadequate—identifying mark. This was my name and phone number written along the white midsole on the inner edge of each shoe. I trusted authorities to take notice if they ever needed this information.

This solution was better than none, but not as effective as others might be. You might want to carry a driver's license or business card, or wear an ID bracelet or necklace, which is vital if you have a medical condition that emergency personnel need to know about immediately.

I don't want to scare anyone, including myself, into thinking that an accident is about to claim you as it did Victoria Place. The odds are overwhelming that no one will ever have to check your identity this way. But it's better to carry ID and never use it than to need it and not have it.

Lesson 17: Checking Technique

Stand alongside a race course sometime and watch a race instead of running it. You'll see in the passing parade some things you might not have noticed from the middle of it. Chances are that you aren't one of the faster runners, and you'll see how wide the gap is between their pace and what yours would be. Chances are even better that you'll notice how different the faster runners look from the runners who are more like you.

Not just pace separates the two groups. They differ even more in appearance. The faster runners glide over the surface, brushing it quickly and quietly with each footfall. They run proudly, with back straight and eyes forward. Faster running almost demands that runners carry themselves in this way.

A slower pace doesn't make such demands, and bad habits can take root. Slower runners are likely to pound the ground, not only spending more time on it but announcing their arrival with an audible slap or scrape. They're likely to run hunched over with eyes cast down, as if they're slightly embarrassed to be there.

Faster runners show us what the best running form should be at any pace. We slower people naturally have a shorter and lower stride but still can model ourselves after those who display the best form. This isn't just advice about looking pretty. Running lightly over the ground, in good head-to-toe alignment, is easier on the body than landing heavily and out of balance a thousand times every mile. Check your form with two tests:

1. **Where do you look?** The back follows the lead of the head. If you watch your feet hit the ground, you're hunched over. But if you raise your eyes to the horizon, your back naturally straightens and you come into more efficient alignment. Good running is straight-backed, tall running.

2. **What do you hear?** The feet announce how well you absorb shock. If you hear slap-slip-scrape-shuffle, you're hitting the ground too hard by not making full use of ankle flex and toe-off. The less you hear at foot plant, the less likely the ground is to hurt you. Good running is springy-stepped, quiet running.

Whatever the pace, run softly, run tall.

Lesson 18: Uphill, Downhill

David Costill, PhD, the sport's leading physiologist, says, "Hilly terrain will significantly impair a runner's performance." Even with an equal amount of climbing and descending, running on hills causes a large net drain on energy compared to flat runs.

You don't need a physiologist (or a poet like Shakespeare, who wrote, "These high, wild hills and rough uneven ways draw out the miles and make them wearisome") to tell you what hills do to your legs and wind. Hills send pulse and breathing rates to their peaks, destroying any value in monitoring breathing and heart rate as controls of effort. Hills, going up and especially coming down, also put extra strain on legs.

When you do run hills, give them the respect they deserve. They shrink for no one, so you have to do the adapting. How do you adapt? By changing your running form. For uphill and downhill running, the form is much different than on flat routes. Adjust for hills the way you would if you were riding a multispeed bicycle on hilly terrain. You know you can't ride all the way up in the same

Hill running requires you to pay attention to and adapt your form to avoid overstressing your legs.

gear. On a bike you have to shift, pump, coast, and brake in tune with the terrain.

Shift to your lower gears while going uphill. Cut stride length. Lean forward. Try to keep the *effort* mostly constant, but not the pace. Speed up without working any harder while going downhill. Lean forward slightly to take advantage of gravity, but stay under control. Don't be too proud to do some braking.

Lesson 19: Style Points

No single running form is right for everyone, but some matters of style are clearly better than others. Check yourself out in the areas listed in table 3.1 to see how close you come to matching the ideal, then try to modify your form in the ways that are open to change.

Table 3.1 Running Styles

Area of concern	Ideal running form
Running posture	Erect with body centered over legs, not leaning forward; back comfortably straight, not hunched; head up and eyes ahead, not looking down
Running footplant	Landing on midfoot, not heel-first; dropping quickly to heel and up again for toe-off, not stiff-ankled; knee slightly flexed, not locked
Running arm action	Hands swinging between waistband and lower chest, not higher or lower; elbows unlocked, not stiff; hands cupped, not tightly clenched or straight-fingered; shoulders low and loose, not high and tight
Running expression	Relaxed and concentrated, not grimacing or with jaw clenched, teeth gritting
Running uphill	Leaning slightly into the hill; pumping harder than normal with arms; lifting more with knees and ankles, but not "fighting" the hill; keep effort fairly constant by slowing the pace somewhat
Running downhill	Absorbing added shock by keeping center of gravity low and landing with exaggerated flex of knees; leaning slightly forward to use gravity; not leaning back or overstriding

Lesson 20: Road Hazards

Streets and roads are convenient places to run, and chances are you do much of your running there. They offer smooth, weatherproof surfaces. In town, streets are lighted for early-morning and late-evening runs. Eventually every runner hits the roads for this convenience and in doing so courts their dangers.

Running in traffic is by far the greatest danger a runner faces. Look at the odds. An automobile weighs more than 10 times as much as you and may travel 10 times as fast. When runner meets car, you know which one wins, regardless of where the fault for the accident lies.

Dozens of runners are maimed or killed in traffic each year, yet runners often overlook the seriousness of the threat. They worry about distance and pace while ignoring the deadly menace hurtling past every few seconds, just an arm's length away. Recognize the risk and exercise these precautions while running on roads:

1. Always yield the right of way. The roads belong to vehicles, if only because of their size, speed, and number. Don't challenge them for space because you'll lose any argument.

2. Run defensively and with a hint of paranoia. Assume that all drivers are out to get you, and don't give them that chance.

3. Stay awake. Runners tend to daydream away the distance, but you can't afford this luxury on a busy street. Keep your head up and your eyes on the road. Consider leaving your personal stereo at home so you can hear what's coming up behind you.

4. Be visible, particularly when running in the dark. Wear brightly colored clothing in the daytime, reflective items at night.

5. See what's coming. Wear a visor or billed cap in darkness to shade your eyes from headlights that could blind you. (Drivers rarely dim their lights for oncoming runners.)

6. Be most careful at sunrise and sunset. Several factors make these the most dangerous hours: rush-hour traffic, sleepy or exhausted commuters, and the glare of the low sun in the drivers' or the runner's eyes.

7. Run on the left, facing traffic—except when that side of the street offers little running room and the right appears safer. On lightly traveled, narrow roads the best path might be down the middle. That way, you can quickly move to either side.

8. Don't forget bicycles and motorcycles. They travel almost as fast as cars, are less visible, and can inflict great damage— both to you and to the rider.

9. Don't provoke drivers by invading their lane, darting out in front of them, or pounding their cars in cases of close calls. You never know when a psycho might be at the wheel.

10. Report serious incidents. Take the license plate number if a driver intentionally swerves to force you off the road or a passenger aims a missile at your head. Runners have charged "assault with a deadly weapon" and won.

Lesson 21: Personal Attacks

The greatest inequity between the sexes is that a man can usually run alone and free of fear almost anywhere at any hour, whereas a lone woman can't go those same places without risking taunts or much worse threats. Men occasionally come under attack. Stories appear every so often in running magazines about a lone male being set upon by young hoodlums with nothing better to do than beat up a defenseless runner. Yet a man on the run is probably safer than he would be if he walked slowly through the same neighborhood. A burst of speed usually leaves the troublemakers behind.

Most attackers choose women as targets for verbal and even physical abuse. These incidents are distressingly common, and their consequences can be quite serious. One women's running club in the Washington, D.C., area reported shocking data on threats and attacks directed at its members. Of 99 women questioned, 41 reported one or more incidents. Most of these were verbal, but more than a quarter of the incidents involved the women being chased or grabbed.

This study listed running areas in order of safety or risk to women. Neighborhoods accounted for 16 percent of the incidents (though most of the running was logged there), while 25 percent occurred on bike paths and 27 percent in secluded parklands (where the least distance was run).

Women fight back in several ways. They run with a partner of either sex or a group, or they carry weapons such as chemical sprays. But perhaps the best solution is to run with a big dog. The dog gets exercise, and you feel safer.

"I haven't had a single comment from a guy since I began running with my Doberman pinscher," says one woman who had been bothered frequently. "The main thing dogs have going for them as partners that people don't is the dog will run at your time and your convenience, your pace, and your distance, without expecting you to carry on witty conversation."

Lesson 22: Running Mates

"The loneliness of the long-distance runner" is a phrase that has endured as a cliché ever since Allan Sillitoe wrote a short novel and later a screenplay by that title in the 1960s. The story was fiction, and so is the applicability of the word lonely to long-distance runners.

Don't feel sorry for the lone runner. This solitude is neither a negative factor nor a necessary evil of the activity. Many runners *prefer* to train by themselves. This may be the only chance they have all day to escape the crowds that press on them, and the voices that assault their ears at home, work, or school. The solitude is self-sought.

Yet a runner who wants this to be a more sociable activity can plug into an active support system. This is among the friendliest of sports—perhaps because there is little person-versus-person competition or because the act of running itself breaks down barriers to communication. Longtime runners will tell you only half-jokingly that running develops one set of muscles more thoroughly than any other—those that operate the mouth. Those same muscles are also the last to tire.

What every runner enjoys most is talking about himself or herself, so you can instantly strike up conversations with strangers who run by asking, "How is your running going?" The most flattering question you can ask a runner is, "Can you give me some advice?" Don't be afraid to ask. Just be prepared for long answers.

Chapter 4
Staying Healthy

Prevent and treat ailments that can interrupt your
training program.

Lesson 23: Health Overview

Governments don't require warning labels on running books and
shoe boxes that read, "Running may be hazardous to your health."
But this activity that undoubtedly promotes health in many ways is
risky in a few others.

Runners don't often suffer the major traumatic injuries of, say, a
skier smacking into a rock, a running back colliding with a line-
backer, or a boxer placing his face against another's fist. Running
injuries usually are minor by comparison—injuries to bone or soft
tissue that don't interfere with daily life but still disrupt training.
That's a runner's definition of injury: anything serious enough to
slow or stop the running. By that standard, a majority of regular
runners can expect to be injured in any given year.

Accidents can happen. You might overlook a pothole, and it
reaches out and sprains an ankle. But most running injuries aren't
accidental. Most result from what doctors call overuse. This is a nice
way of saying we make mistakes in training and racing, which is
another way of saying the problems of runners are largely self-
inflicted. We can't blame fate or others, only ourselves. Injury is one
penalty we pay for running too far, too fast, and too often. (Coming

down with stress-related illnesses such as colds or the flu is another penalty.) It's nature's reminder to cut back somewhere.

Within this depressing statement of risk factors we can find two pieces of good news:

• Because these ailments occur for predictable reasons, they are generally quite treatable. Find the cause and correct it, and relief is likely to follow. Make this correction permanent, and the condition is unlikely to recur.

• Because running injuries are usually minor, at least when treated early, very few of them require medical intervention or become long-term disruptions. Even fewer of these breakdowns force runners to become ex-runners.

Lesson 24: Getting Hurt

A running injury doesn't usually strike with sudden and devastating consequences like a compound fracture of the leg. These problems are more in the nature of slow, steady erosion that wears down the body. The physical pain of most running injuries is rarely severe, hurting less than an average headache or toothache, if at all. However, a sore spot the size of a fingerprint can be debilitating when you put three times your body weight on it—which is the average force of a running step.

Running-injury surveys report the following injury facts:

- The weakest link in runners is the knee. About one in five injured runners has a knee problem.
- Nearly as many runners undergo a breakdown in the Achilles tendon, the thin band of tissue connecting the heel bone with the calf muscles.
- About 10 percent suffer shinsplints, an imprecise term covering ailments in the front of the lower leg and ranging from tendinitis to stress fractures.
- Forefoot strains and stress fractures, severe heel pain, and damage to the arch each account for a significant portion of injuries, though fewer than 10 percent of runners suffer from any of these ailments.

There isn't enough space here to diagnose and treat each injury. It is better that we talk about why these injuries happen, in hopes of reducing the high toll. Injuries occur for four main reasons:

1. Overwork—too much training and racing for the feet and legs to handle, causing the weakest link to break.
2. Faulty equipment—usually meaning shoes that are either inadequate for the purpose or are worn beyond their useful limit.
3. Weakness or inflexibility—muscles that are so overspecialized that the slightest unusual twist (a sudden increase in speed, a run over uneven or hilly ground) strains them.
4. Mechanical problems—either faults in running form or the way the foot meets the ground (which can be corrected with a specially made shoe insert).

While treating the symptoms of injury, you should also do some detective work into causes. Look to adjusted workloads, well-made and well-maintained shoes, supplemental strength-stretch exercises, and mechanical improvements for permanent cures.

Lesson 25: Getting Sick

Running can make you sick, but it can also act as preventive medicine or an aid to treatment. It all depends on how you use it or abuse it. Runners can either build resistance to certain illnesses or erode it. You're constantly exposed, for instance, to the viruses that cause colds and the flu. Yet these illnesses surface only after stress has eroded the body's natural defenses.

Evidence gleaned from several scientific studies indicates that runners as a group suffer fewer colds than nonrunners. This may have to do with increased body heat that may destroy some of the viruses. Runners also notice that the congestion of a cold clears up quicker if they run during the cold's waning stages.

However, continued hard running while experiencing the early symptoms can turn a mild cold into a dreadful one and may lead to side effects such as a lingering case of bronchitis. Catching cold means you already have worked too hard. Don't compound the problem.

George Sheehan, MD, the longtime and legendary medical columnist for *Runner's World* magazine, spent a large part of each day advising ailing runners. Here's a summary of his advice for treating the two most common illnesses:

• **Colds.** "I treat them with respect. It is my feeling that they represent a breakdown of the defense system. The cold is an early-warning symptom of exhaustion." Sheehan advised following the body's warnings and cut back, or even cut out, training for the first one to

When you're feeling sick, take it easy. Pay attention to what your body is telling you.

three days of the cold, "then resume at a slow pace for relatively short distances. However, do not wait until all symptoms subside." Start running to clear away the cold's debris.

• **Flu.** The flu's most worrisome symptom is fever. "Don't run with a fever!" warned Dr. Sheehan. "After that, as a rule of thumb, take two days easy for each day of fever. A week of fever and symptoms, therefore, would call for an additional two weeks' recovery period. Exhausting runs should be avoided at this time, or recurrence is a distinct possibility." Sheehan added, "When you come back, it is difficult to know whether fatigue is physical or psychological. There is, however, a simple test for this. Start your runs very slowly until you start to sweat. This usually takes about six minutes. At this point, you should feel like running—no matter how you felt at the beginning. If you don't and five more minutes confirms it, pack it in for that day." Exhaustion is the common denominator in these illnesses, and avoiding it is the best medicine.

Running Commentary: Trial Mile

This isn't to suggest that all Kenyans train all the time in the way I'll describe. But one of them, Cosmas Ndeti, showed me this way at a time when I most needed direction. The *New York Times* carried a profile on him in 1995, including these lines: "He runs according to the way he feels each morning, not according to any rigid schedule. He has been known to wake up, run for a kilometer, then climb back into bed."

At the time I was slogging through one of my frequent spells of Achilles tendinitis. It had stayed with me for weeks without improving, as I'd tried to meet a prearranged schedule of half-hour "easy" runs that still were too hard on my heel.

Taking a clue from Ndeti, I listened more closely to what the Achilles told me each morning. Because miles and not meters is my first language, I ran a single mile (1.6 kilometers) and then decided what, if anything, to do next. The Achilles injury limited me to that one mile at first. But soon the tendon announced that it was beginning to heal quickly under this gentler treatment. Within a few weeks I was ready for a half marathon race—a slow one, to be sure, but on a pain-free foot.

As soon as the healing was complete, though, I fell back into the old routine. I forgot that therapeutic trick and resumed a rigid schedule—always a half-hour run on easy days. Predictably, the hurting returned in a different incarnation.

I've now resurrected that plan to make the easy days easier: Run one mile (or 10 minutes on the watch if you're a time runner like me), then decide whether to go on or go home. If the signs of trouble appear or don't clear, and especially if they intensify, forgo the extra mile(s). Call it an early day, and try for more tomorrow. If this warm-up/test says to continue, run one more mile and make the same decision again. Keep going only as long as the running remains easy and pain-free, which might be one mile or one hour that day.

Why, you might ask, even bother with this mile? Why not just decide whether to run before dressing and going out the door? The answer has to do with listening to your body. The advisers all tell you to do this, but they rarely say *when* to listen most closely. Before the run isn't the right time. That's when the body likes to tell its biggest lies—trying to convince you that it feels better or worse than it really does.

Sometimes running injuries go into hibernation between runs. You tell yourself at the start that you're okay, you try to run as planned, you overdo, the pain comes out of hiding, and you suffer a recovery setback by not stopping soon enough.

Just as often, though, the problem feels worst when you're not running. You think before starting that you're hurting and need another day off. A warm-up might work out the stiffness and soreness.

The trial mile acts as a truth serum. It tells honestly what you're able to do that day. Listen.

Lesson 26: Recovery Road

An injury has knocked you off your feet. What to do now? Whatever the specifics of your malady, there is a path back to health that lets you heal and still stay somewhat active. If you can't run steadily, mix walking and running. If all running is impossible, just walk. Or if walking hurts too much, bike or swim. Choose your level of activity according to the severity of symptoms listed in table 4.1.

Table 4.1   Comeback Trail

If you feel this ...	Try this activity ...
Walking is painful, running is impossible.	Bike or swim for usual running time periods. These activities take nearly all pressure off most injuries, while still giving steady workouts. They make you feel that you still have some control over your physical life.
Walking is relatively pain-free, running still hurts.	Start to walk as soon as you can move ahead without limping. Continue as long as pain doesn't become intolerable. (These limitations apply at all stages of recovery.)
Walking is easy, and some running is possible.	As walks become too easy, add intervals of slow running—as little as one minute in five at first, then gradually building up the amount of running until you reach the next stage.
Running pain eases, but minor discomfort persists.	The balance tips in favor of running mixed with walking. Insert brief walks at this stage when you can't yet tolerate steady pressure.
All pain and tenderness is blessedly gone.	Run again, but approach it cautiously for a while as you regain lost fitness. Run a little slower than normal, with no long or fast efforts until you can handle the short-slow runs comfortably.

Lesson 27: Stress Loads

The human body and mind create a symphony. Some of the individual instruments boom, others whisper. Together they make melodies, harmonies, and rhythms. When the individual parts blend as intended, you don't hear them as separate elements. You hear the musical whole, and it's beautiful. But a single instrument out of tune can destroy the music and make you painfully aware of the discord.

Stresses are normal and natural parts of living, and you can't escape them—you can only work with them. They come from many

When recovering from an injury allow yourself an easier pace.

directions and in various combinations. The runner doesn't move through a vacuum. The act of running is only one of many stresses acting on a runner. At least seven families of stresses combine to produce a single result: the draining of adaptation reserves. The major stresses and examples of each are as follows:

1. Work—specific stress of running, and general stresses of day's physical and mental labor
2. Emotional—anxiety, depression, anger
3. Social—isolation, overcrowding

4. Dietary—too much, too little, or wrong type of food
5. Rest—inadequate recovery from hard work, sleep deprivation
6. Health—injury, illness, infection
7. Environmental—heat and cold, high altitude, air pollution

We absorb these stresses into the pace of life. They become obvious and harmful only when they come in too-heavy amounts for too long a period. Then off-key notes stand out. The signs and symptoms of overstress are easy to spot (see Lesson 29, page 48). If detected early and analyzed correctly, they can be reduced before they do serious damage. But if overall stress loads remain high, they lead to physical or psychological failure.

Think of yourself as a violin string. Like the string, you have a great creative capacity. But that potential is wasted when you lie limp and unused. Only when you're stretched are you filling your intended role. Yet the stretching can go too far. When pressures pull too hard in opposite directions, *snap!*

Your task as a runner is to find a point of stretch, a level of activity, that expresses your talent while holding resiliency in reserve. When emergencies come up—either real or artificial, in the form of hard training and racing—you should be able to meet them by stretching more instead of snapping.

Lesson 28: Preventive Medicine

Hans Selye, MD, was never a serious runner, yet the Canadian physiologist provided a basis for modern running training with his general adaptation syndrome (GAS) theory. Selye said that stress is "quite simple to understand. It is essentially the wear and tear in the body caused by life at any one time."

A person exposed to stress (running is one stress among the many noted in the previous list) erects defenses to counteract it. The body has a reservoir of adaptive energy for handling everyday battering, plus a reserve supply for emergencies. If the stress is applied in small, regular doses, the body adapts to it by growing stronger. But if the doses are too heavy and prolonged, the body can't cope. The reserves are drained, and the person goes into the exhaustion phase of the syndrome, becoming highly susceptible to breakdowns.

This is when the discordant notes surface: sudden drops in performance, drastic weight loss, rapid pulse, disturbed sleep, carryover fatigue from one day to the next, colds or fever, anxiety or irritability, pain. According to Selye, adaptation energy resembles a special kind of bank account that we can use by making withdrawals but cannot replace fully with deposits. We can't keep drawing on this stress account indefinitely without paying a penalty in depleted reserves.

So how does this theory translate into practical terms for a runner—avoid stress? Not at all. If you're going to improve your running, you must court a specific type of stress. The trick in training is to run enough to build up but not so much that you tear down. This same exercise can be either helpful or hurtful, depending on how you decide to apply it. The art of training is determining just the right amount.

Selye concluded, "The goal is certainly not to avoid stress. Stress is part of life. It is a natural by-product of all-out activities. But in order to express yourself fully, you must find your optimum stress level. . . . It is not easy. It takes much practice and constant self-analysis."

Lesson 29: Warning Signs

The signs of adaptive success and failure are readily detectable. Improved performance, accompanied by pain-free running, means you're adapting nicely to this stress. However, as you approach the exhausted state, your body and mind send out danger signals. These include persistent soreness and stiffness, nervousness, and many others.

This variety of signals tell us when we're in or out of tune. It's a wise runner who develops a sensitive ear to the body's signals. By reading and interpreting these signs, he or she can go a long way toward stopping trouble at its source.

The damage doesn't often happen at random, without an obvious explanation. Athletic ailments aren't punishment from wrathful gods but are predictable results of too much work and too little attention to clear warning signs.

In 1966, Tom Osler published the greatest piece of literature, page for page, in the history of running. His 32-page pamphlet, *The Conditioning of Distance Runners*, packed together more helpful hints than subsequent books 10 times its size. Osler listed a set of minor early-warning signs that if heeded could prevent most of the major injuries and illnesses that strike runners. These physical and mental symptoms of overstress tell you to apply the brakes and ease down your efforts until the road clears.

This list of the 10 surest signs of too much stress is adapted from Osler's original list. Treat each of these signs as a friendly warning that you may be running toward a crash.

1. Resting pulse rate significantly higher than normal when taken before getting out of bed in the morning
2. Difficulty falling asleep and staying asleep
3. Sores in and around the mouth, and other skin eruptions in nonadolescents
4. Any symptoms of a cold or the flu—sniffles, sore throat, or fever
5. Swollen, tender glands in the neck, groin, or underarms—sure signs that the body is fighting infection
6. Labored breathing during even the mildest of daily runs
7. Dizziness or nausea before, during, or after running
8. Clumsiness—for instance, tripping or kicking yourself during a run over rather smooth ground
9. Any muscle or tendon pain, or stiffness that remains after the first few minutes of a run
10. No feeling of anticipation before running and no feeling of accomplishment afterward, as dread and depression become the dominant emotions

Chapter 5

Eating Right

Learn which foods, drinks, and supplements
contribute the most to your running fitness.

Lesson 30: Diet Overview

No one argues with the premise that eating right is fundamental to good health. The argument is over what's "right." So divergent are the various nutritional opinions that you're left wondering what to think. You can't believe everything you read on the subject, because conflict and confusion dot this literary landscape.

Our discussion isn't meant to summarize in a few pages a topic that fills whole bookcases. The plan here is to shortcut past the nutritional battlefields and find areas of general agreement on what works best for runners.

Work on eating well, to be sure. But don't think that you will improve your running simply by improving your diet. No magic comes by mouth. At best, nutrition has an indirect effect on your fitness. Better eating and drinking habits promote better health, which clears the way to better training, which only then lets you run better.

You might do your running a bigger favor by taking something out of your diet than by adding a new ingredient. Rather than searching for miracle pills and potions, eat less in total and drop some weight, and cut down on the fats, simple sugars, and alcohol. Identify and eliminate items that cause intolerance reactions. Try running on empty or nearly so instead of training or racing too soon after a meal.

As for added items, the preferred fuels for runners are rich in complex carbohydrates. Carbo loading has a proud history of helping runners before marathons, and now the practice has found wider favor—for reloading after races and hard workouts and for extending energy supplies by eating during a run. In other words, these foods taste good and do good most of the time.

Drinks also serve a body well almost anytime. The drink that does you the most good with the fewest complications is the simplest one: water.

Lesson 31: Your Cravings

For many years after launching his running and sports medicine careers in the 1960s, Dr. George Sheehan paid little attention in his columns and speeches to dietary matters. But his readers and listeners wouldn't let the subject rest. So his thinking and writing and speaking about it increased. In his later work he brought a refreshing mixture of belief and skepticism on this topic too often weighted down with dogma.

For instance, due to their abuse, sugars and fats have been given bad names in the medical, dental, nutritional, and fitness communities. Sheehan had kinder words for these substances than did many of his colleagues, who often make sugar and fat sound like poison. While Sheehan the doctor preferred that carbohydrate needs be filled mostly from more natural, complex sources, Sheehan the athlete knew the appetites of a person in training.

"Apparently, this is the diet that runners' instincts tell them is best. As their mileage increases, so does their need for quick-energy 'junk food,'" he said. Vigorous exercise "affects the 'appestat.' This is the instinct that tells us what, when, and how much to eat. The thermostat-like system shuts down when we sit around too much, but exercise keeps it working." Our cravings for sugar and starch signal that the appestat is working.

Sheehan listed his own top two dietary rules: "First, I must carry the least weight possible. Second, I must have the most available energy possible. The first must be accomplished without losing strength, the second without gaining weight." This would be a hard line to walk if not for the automatic appestat telling us what, when, and how much to eat.

Fat has long been portrayed as the enemy of the fit. This has been accepted as true for both fat worn on the body as excess baggage and fat taken in as food. So exercisers have leaned toward lightness in what they eat and what they carry. They've sometimes leaned too far.

Sheehan favored leanness but warned against extreme skinniness. He reported a study of ballet dancers who trained six to eight hours a day—far more than a runner would train. Their casualty rate from bone, muscle, and tendon injuries was high. The researchers found that the dancers most prone to injury were those on diets that held them below 2,000 calories a day. The healthiest were those who ate what their appetites requested.

The exercising body demands its prime energy sources—lots of carbohydrates and small but regular amounts of fat. These food-stuffs are the very same ones a dieter tries to eliminate first as "too fattening" and are the first to be missed.

Lesson 32: Eating Wrong

Runners operate under physical and sometimes emotional stress and strain. This temporarily stressful situation makes runners peculiarly susceptible to diet-related irregularities that might not strike people who operate on a lower plane of activity. There are two main causes of internal distress:

• **Eating too much, too late, before running**. We run best on an empty or nearly empty stomach. Arthur Lydiard, the prominent coach from New Zealand, observed that runners rarely collapse from malnutrition during a run. They do have problems of the opposite type—doubling over with side pains called stitches, making pit stops along the way (few runners ever complain about irregularity), or simply running with an unpleasant sloshing and bloated feeling. Eat lightly, if at all, in the last hours before running. Your body holds abundant stored energy to carry you through.

- **Eating the wrong foods at the wrong times**. Some of us can't tolerate certain food groups and may react violently to them—particularly in times of stress. Surprisingly, two chief culprits may be two of the most basic—milk and bread. Sheehan said a great number of his pleas for help come from runners who don't tolerate milk and bread products very well. He identified other suspect foods as the highly allergenic ones (chocolate and shellfish are two) and excessive fiber (raw fruits and vegetables, whole grains). Even if you

In addition to running for better health, you also must eat a variety of healthful foods.

don't have a specific intolerance, you're wise to avoid most or all of these items—along with anything heavy in fat, which digests slowly—in the last meal before a run, and especially before a race.

There is one basic rule in these two areas: Err on the side of too little rather than too much. And when in doubt about eating something, *don't.*

Lesson 33: Weight Watching

Nutritional advisors tell you to find your proper weight and then maintain it. But arriving at the ideal figure, either pinpointing it or achieving it, isn't as easy as it sounds. One method is to labor through a lengthy trial-and-error process of measuring weight against performance. Another way is to consult a standard weight chart, which almost invariably lets you weigh too much. Yet another, and the best, method is to measure your body-fat percentage. This is the most accurate measure of ideal body composition (ideals are 12 to 15 percent for men and 18 to 22 percent for women), but it is a technique not readily available to most of us.

So we're left with rough rules of thumb that apply to people of average build but don't take into account the vast differences in frame sizes. One such estimate comes from Irwin Maxwell Stillman, MD, author of a number of diet books. In his formula, men start from a base of 110 pounds, then add 5.5 pounds for every inch of height above five feet. A man six feet tall, for instance, adds 66 pounds for a target weight of 176 pounds. (In meters, this formula starts from a base of 50 kilograms at 1.60 meters and adds about one kilogram for each additional centimeter.)

Women start from 100 pounds under the Stillman formula. They add five pounds for each inch over five feet. A five-foot-five woman, then, is allowed 125 pounds. (Metrically, the base figure is 45 kilograms at 1.60 meters, with the addition of about 0.8 kilogram for each added centimeter.)

Stillman added, "If you're an athlete [of either sex], it's best to weigh about five pounds [2.2 kilograms] less than the ideal weight listed."

Running does burn calories, of course, but not as quickly as you might suspect. The average figure generally quoted is 100 calories per mile (1.6 kilometers). At that rate you must run 10 miles (16 kilometers) or more to get rid of that milk shake you drank last night. You must run 35 miles to drop a single pound (or about 120 kilometers to shed one kilogram)—and that is assuming you eat nothing new in the meantime.

If you plan to lose weight by running, you must accept the fact that you'll take it off gradually. Suppose you're running two or three miles (three to five kilometers) three or four days a week, while keeping your intake constant. That effort equals about 1,000 calories a week, so you can plan on losing a pound (0.4 kilogram) every three weeks. In a year's time this may amount to a significant 15 pounds (nearly seven kilograms). With dietary limitations, the timetable may be speeded up.

But heed this warning: Resist the temptation to indulge in quick-loss schemes. These usually involve artificial water-weight drops along with declines in energy. The first item you cut out while dieting is high-carbohydrate foods such as grains, potatoes, and sugars—the same items you need to sustain running. Excessive sweating from running in heavy clothing may take off weight quickly, but this weight doesn't stay lost. Think of weight reduction as a long-term project that will be permanent on completion.

Running Commentary: Pills for Ills

My first meal of the day includes a multiple-vitamin tablet. I don't believe wholeheartedly in the benefits of this one pill, but I take it anyway just to be safe. I routinely swallow no other supplements the rest of the day, which makes me something of a conservative among runners.

Rare is the runner who believes that the normal American diet fulfills all nutritional needs. A thriving industry serves athletes who are convinced that they can enhance health and fitness with pills and potions. They believe in popping something for whatever ails them—from headaches and stomach upsets to physical fatigue and mental dullness. For runners, the supplements fall into five categories. They range from special foods to serious drugs:

1. **Foods.** Sports bars, gels, and drinks promise to increase energy and improve recovery. Runners consume products such as PowerBars,

GU gel, and Gatorade before, after, and during their long training sessions and races. They wake up with caffeine in one of its liquid forms.

2. **Herbs.** Ginseng is marketed as an endurance enhancer and is the main ingredient in the popular supplement Endurox. Echinacea and other herbal products are reputed to protect against viral infections. Saint-John's-wort supposedly brightens the mood, and ginkgo biloba allegedly sharpens the mind.

3. **Vitamins, minerals, etc.** Dr. Kenneth Cooper, a founding father of running for fitness, urges all exercisers to take a combination of antioxidants—vitamins C and E, plus beta-carotene. Women runners are thought to need increased amounts of iron and calcium. Glucosamine may strengthen the joints, and creatine may bulk up the muscles.

4. **Fully legal drugs.** Pain relievers such as aspirin and its substitutes, including acetaminophen (found in Tylenol) and ibuprofen (found in Advil), are available without a doctor's prescription. Some runners think they need to down these pills to get through a workout or race.

5. **Semilegal drugs.** Some over-the-counter drugs are clearly banned by athletic governing bodies. These drugs include DHEA and andro (androstenedione), which act like a steroid or testosterone to boost strength. Others are legal in low amounts but banned in excessive quantities, such as the common congestion reliever ephedrine, and even caffeine.

Some of these products work as promised. Sports bars and gels, for instance, can significantly delay or even eliminate late-race letdowns in marathons. Aspirinlike products do relieve pain, masking it temporarily while leaving its cause untreated. A little caffeine gives a prerun lift.

The semilegal drugs work, but possibly at a physical or ethical price. Athletes are banned from using them out of concern over the long-term side effects and because they give an unfair competitive advantage.

Most of the supplements that runners take are less dramatic in their benefits as well as their side effects. Scientific testing on the benefits of vitamin, mineral, and herbal preparations is inconclusive at best. This lack of absolute proof doesn't turn runners away from these products. They work because we use the strongest additive of all—faith.

Lesson 34: Water Weight

Though weight loss from dehydration is temporary, it's still vitally important to runners. The significant effects of dehydration are negative, ranging from impaired performance to heat collapse. Here, in simplest terms, is what happens. A quart of sweat weighs about two pounds (a liter, about a kilogram), and a runner can lose that much before noticing any ill effects. As the deficit grows, body temperature rises proportionately, pushing toward a critical level.

C.H. Wyndham, a South African, has done extensive research on heat responses. He said, "Up to a water deficit of about three percent body temperature varies between about 101 and 102 degrees [Fahrenheit, or about 38° Celsius]. But with an increase in water deficit above three percent rectal temperatures increased in proportion to the extent of water deficit."

The two- or three-degree F (one to two degrees C) rise is normal and acceptable for a runner. But increases beyond that point bear watching. American physiologist David Costill has measured sweat losses as great as 10 percent in marathon runners and temperatures as high as 105 degrees F (40° C). Body heat only slightly higher than that can lead to heat exhaustion or heatstroke, the latter being potentially fatal. (Don't be alarmed here. You're unlikely to overheat during your comfortably paced daily runs.)

Drinking immediately before, during, and after runs won't completely eliminate losses. But it can replace enough of the lost fluid and cool the temperatures to a degree where exercise is at least safe. Dr. Costill said runners tend to let the sensation of thirst set their drinking habits, and thirst sometimes fibs about true fluid needs. "In laboratory tests that required about eight pounds of sweat loss," said Costill, "we found that thirst was temporarily satisfied by drinking as little as one pound of water."

Water accounts for nearly all of the loss and is the replacement drink of choice because it is absorbed quickly, with few or no complications. After a heavy sweat loss it may take several days to redress the balance, and chronic dehydration may result from repeated heavy drains and inadequate replacement. The best way to guard against this is to check your weight each day. If you're down more than two pounds (or one kilogram) from the day before, you're a quart (or liter) low on liquids. Drink up!

Drinking plenty of fluids isn't important only during a race. You need to consume an adequate amount of water daily.

Lesson 35: Sweat Debt

Fluid losses exceeding 3 percent of body weight represent significant dehydration. Table 5.1 translates the 3 percent figure into pounds and kilograms for runners of various sizes. Pre- and postrun weight checks are recommended, especially after hard runs and in hot, humid weather. Take the most accurate reading of your sweat debt by weighing yourself right after the run—before drinking heavily or eating at all. Restore all of the water-weight loss before running again.

Table 5.1 Weighing In

Prerun in pounds (kilograms)	Postrun in pounds (kilograms)
100 (45)	97 (44)
105 (48)	102 (46)
110 (50)	107 (48)
115 (52)	112 (51)
120 (54)	116 (53)
125 (57)	121 (55)
130 (59)	126 (57)
135 (61)	131 (59)
140 (64)	136 (62)
145 (66)	141 (64)
150 (68)	145 (66)
155 (70)	150 (68)
160 (73)	155 (70)
165 (75)	160 (73)
170 (77)	165 (75)
175 (79)	170 (77)
180 (82)	175 (79)
185 (84)	180 (82)
190 (86)	184 (84)
195 (89)	189 (86)
200 (91)	194 (88)

Lesson 36: Running Fuel

German doctor/coach/researcher Ernst van Aaken once remarked, "No one ever got fast by eating." Yet as coach Arthur Lydiard pointed out, "The way runners eat before races, you'd think they were worried about dying of malnutrition after 50 meters."

Dr. van Aaken thought runners should eat little or nothing 12 hours before a race. They have all the stored fuel they need, he asserted, and putting more food into a tense system might cause indigestion, cramping, diarrhea, or other difficulties. Van Aaken and Lydiard agreed that the final hours before a race is too late for the food to do much good, but not too late for it to do harm.

The prerace week is another matter. Significant benefits come from carbohydrate loading during this period. This technique involves packing the body with high-energy fuel called glycogen, a product of foods rich in carbohydrates. The theory behind carbo loading is that muscle glycogen supplies are limited and are depleted in long races, causing us to slow down or stop. But we can build up these reserves by juggling carbo intake, and we can then go farther before smacking into a wall. The diet does not increase speed; it only delays slowing. It works best in runs and races lasting longer than two hours, the point at which glycogen depletion would normally reach a critical stage.

The classic carbo-loading routine encompasses three stages:

1. The long "depletion" run seven days before the competition to drain the runner of glycogen
2. The protein phase—three days of keeping the glycogen level low by eating high-protein, low-carbohydrate meals (meats, eggs, fish, and the like)
3. The carbohydrate phase—three days of packing in the carbos (bread, pasta, rice)

Runners' major complaint about the routine involves the high-protein phase. They say they feel exhausted, irritable, and susceptible to illness and loss of confidence at the worst possible time. A modified version of the carbo-loading routine gives some of the benefits while reducing the risks. They simply take a medium-length depletion run about four days before the race, then start carbo loading immediately.

Carbohydrate maintenance during the run and reloading after are at least as important as the initial loading. Carbo levels are already relatively high going into a long run, but the draining begins right away. Runners can partly overcome this by consuming an energy bars or gel for athletes. Research has shown that consuming high-carbo drinks and foods in the first hour after finishing a run or race speeds recovery.

PART II
Running for Fitness

The answers to the big questions of running logistics vary enormously, but every runner needs to address them: How far? How fast? How often? Reverse their order, change the words, and they spell FIT—frequency, intensity, and time.

Chapter 6
Personalizing Training

Plug in your answers to three key questions:
How far? How fast? How often?

Lesson 37: Training Overview

Although answers to the big questions of running logistics vary enormously, every runner needs to consider how far, how fast, and how often to run. To get the answers, think FIT—frequency, intensity, and time.

- Frequency is how often you run. Every other day is the generally accepted minimum standard for gaining and maintaining basic fitness. Habitual runners, however, usually choose to run most days of the week. Ambitious runners don't stop at seven weekly workouts but train twice most of those days. How well you recover from one run to the next determines your ideal frequency.

- **Intensity is how fast you run**. Pushing the pace is sometimes required of runners training to race. But speedwork must be treated as a prescription item taken in small, well-spaced doses. Even the top runners must run easily much of the time. "Easy" and "hard" are better terms than "slow" and "fast," because someone else's easy pace per mile or kilometer might feel racelike to you. How comfortable the run feels is the best gauge of ideal intensity.

- **Time is how long you run**. Time is an easier way to check the length of runs than distance because you don't have to measure a course, or stick to a set route, or convert from miles to kilometers while traveling. All you need to do is check your watch. Most fitness benefits come in the first half hour, but going longer can provide benefits in such areas as race training as well as relaxation and meditation. What you want from running will set the ideal length of your sessions.

Lesson 38: Training Plans

Where, you deserve to know, did the training ideas outlined in most of the remaining chapters originate? Who laid the foundation and what are their credentials? The names Bill Bowerman, Kenneth Cooper, and Arthur Lydiard loomed largest in the first running boom that began in the late 1960s and peaked in the mid-'70s. By changing the training techniques and attitudes that had previously dominated running, these three giants helped make it possible for running to be more than a sport for elite young athletes (nearly all of them male).

Bowerman was a renowned track coach at the University of Oregon who had trained more sub-four-minute milers than any other American. He traveled to New Zealand in the early 1960s and met Lydiard, an even more prominent coach who had developed two gold medalists at the Rome Olympics. Bowerman was most impressed that Lydiard had introduced thousands of New Zealanders of all ages and abilities to running. Bowerman began to run when he returned home, and thousands of Americans soon followed his lead.

Lydiard, a onetime marathon runner himself, abandoned the track-oriented training methods of his era in favor of extensive distance running on roads. Then he translated this system into schedules that nonelite runners could use. Track runners who trained on roads eventually gravitated to racing longer distances there, which led to the boom in this branch of the sport.

Cooper had been a high school and college runner. While serving in the air force, he tested hundreds of thousands of military personnel for their reactions to exercise. He concluded that steady, prolonged aerobic-type activity was most beneficial and that running was the most efficient of these exercises. His first book, *Aerobics*, which was first published in 1968 and has been updated several times since, won millions of converts to running.

Lesson 39: Training Tips

Other authorities—Tom Osler and Jeff Galloway head the list from more recent years, and you'll hear from them in later chapters—added to and refined the Cooper-Lydiard-Bowerman ideas. But your training programs as outlined in this book stand firmly on the foundation built by the three geniuses who revolutionized this activity.

- **Cover at least 10 minutes, or about one mile (1.6 kilometers).** According to Kenneth Cooper, you must run about 10 minutes before you achieve any training benefit. The three experts agree that this is a bare-minimum running time, so you start at this level—as either a

With proper training you will be able to run faster and farther.

warm-up for experienced runners or a full session for beginners—and work up from here.

• **Use the "talk test."** This is Bill Bowerman's term. He said if you can talk while you run, you're doing fine. If you're gasping, you're going too fast. (A higher-tech and more exact alternative is heart-rate monitoring.)

• **Train, don't strain**. This is Arthur Lydiard's catchphrase. Running should not be exhausting, particularly at this early stage but also on most days for advanced runners. Lydiard said you should rarely go beyond the limits of "pleasant tiredness."

• **Run by time**. Lydiard encouraged runners to concern themselves only with time periods, not with distances, on most of their runs. You can rush a measured distance in order to finish it sooner, but time can't be hurried along, so you're more likely to run your minutes at a comfortable, safe pace.

• **Employ intervals if necessary**. This is another Bowerman tip (refined and promoted later by Tom Osler and Jeff Galloway). Start the exercise period with the intention of running as much of it as you can, remembering to keep it aerobic and unstrained. If breathing becomes labored or pains set in, slow to a walk until you feel recovered, then resume running. Repeat as required, and take as long as necessary to fill the day's quota of running minutes.

• **Rest and recover**. Bowerman employed the "hard-easy" principle. He said no one he ever coached could work hard every day and continue to improve. Progress comes most quickly, he noted, when you alternate days of effort with days of recovery. This could mean running every other day (resting or cross-training in between), or alternating harder and easier runs.

• **Challenge yourself occasionally**. All three experts were competitive runners who recognized the motivational values of racing. They all built tests of one form or another into their programs to add excitement. For you, tests could be true races, time trials, or simply runs that are a little longer or faster than normal.

Running Commentary: Running Around

Progress doesn't necessarily run in a straight line, angling upward over time, forever breaking new ground, always finding better ways. We can also progress by traveling in a full circle. My life's running course is clearly circular.

T.S. Eliot once wrote, "The end to all our exploring will be to arrive at where we started—and to know the place for the first time." I add to that: Most of what I needed to know, I knew before knowing hardly anything. That is, early instincts told me what to do as a runner, and time has proven them correct. These instincts pointed me the right ways in my running and split it into three parts. By arrival date they are: fast, easy, and long.

• **Fast**. My first timed distance run was a mile (1.6 kilometers) at age 10. My first high school distance race, four years later, was a mile.

• **Easy**. My first easy runs took me to the checkerboard squares of farmland outside of town. These blocks were a mile per side, or four miles (about 6 1/2 kilometers) for a complete circuit, or about a half hour of running.

• **Long**. My first long runs were away from school. The road between my high school and my home stretched about eight miles (13 kilometers) and took an hour or so to run.

The early mix of long, fast, and easy—as primitive as it might seem now—led to a handful of high school state titles. But not knowing how much I knew from the start caused me to wander far from these practices while looking for something better. Between entering college in the early 1960s and entering middle age in the mid-1980s, I went to all-fast running, then all-long, and finally all-easy. The all-fast phase exhausted me, the all-long injured me, and the all-easy bored me.

If progress takes a great circle route back to the starting point, I stood farthest away from it during the phase of nothing but easy half-hour runs. This period, ending in 1987, was when my running was most unbalanced. Gone was two-thirds of what had attracted me to running. Longer runs returned first. I sometimes ran two and even three hours while preparing for an occasional marathon. But my norm went back to what it had been when I first ran the eight miles home from school as a teenager. One hour was then, and is now, the longest run for most weeks.

Faster runs returned later. Mile races are old memories now, but out alone some mornings I run one-and-ones—one mile, at least one minute faster than the pace I run on the other days—to remind myself of the effort required at this distance that I raced first and most often.

Easy runs are again gap fillers between long and fast. The easy ones carry me back to the days when I ran around the four-mile country blocks in Iowa. In all three ways—long, fast, and easy—I'm back to where I started. And I finally know how these runs relate to each other and what they mean to me.

Lesson 40: How Far?

Run long enough, but not too long. Most experts agree that most of running's physical benefits can be accomplished with 15- to 30-minute runs. You certainly can keep your body reasonably fit on a few miles or kilometers a day, a few days a week.

However, another doctor reminds us that the body also has a head attached, and the mind has its own different requirements. Psychiatrist Thaddeus Kostrubala, MD, is as much a pioneer as Cooper, having used running as a therapeutic tool for a decade. Dr. Kostrubala said his patients complained of feeling terrible early in their runs. But if he nursed them through these doldrums and the runs lasted a half hour or more, the symptoms improved. The most productive therapy sessions followed the longer runs, said Kostrubala.

Mentally healthy runners experience the same pattern. The early minutes aren't often pleasant, even for fit athletes who have run for years. This is a time for warming up and for finding your running rhythm. Runners wade through the early stage so they can get to the good part, which may not arrive until a half hour has passed.

For this reason you're advised to fit your run into at least a 30-minute period. You do this because the longer periods are more satisfying. They warm you up; they give you time to think and to work off disturbing thoughts and tensions. Walking can occupy much of the total time at first, but work toward running comfortably for an uninterrupted half hour or more in all your sessions.

Experienced runners typically spend most of their days in the 30- to 60-minute time frame. This is long enough to be rewarding but short enough to remain good, healthy fun and not become a second job; long enough to make you want to come back for more and short enough to allow you to do so. Runs in this range fulfill the enthusiasm needs without draining the energy pool.

For reasons of practicality (see Lesson 14, page 24) this book recommends measuring most runs by time periods instead of distances. But runners still like to know about how far they've run. To convert your times, estimate your average pace per mile (or kilometer) for the appropriate time period and find your distance in table 6.1.

Table 6.1 Training Distances

Pace per mile (km)	Distance in miles (km) in 30 minutes	Distance in miles (km) in 60 minutes
6:00 (3:44)	5.0 (8.0)	10.0 (16.1)
6:30 (4:02)	4.6 (7.4)	9.2 (14.8)
7:00 (4:20)	4.3 (6.9)	8.6 (13.8)
7:30 (4:39)	4.0 (6.4)	8.0 (12.9)
8:00 (4:58)	3.8 (6.1)	7.5 (12.1)
8:30 (5:17)	3.5 (5.7)	7.1 (11.4)
9:00 (5:35)	3.3 (5.3)	6.7 (10.8)
9:30 (5:53)	3.1 (5.0)	6.3 (10.1)
10:00 (6:12)	3.0 (4.8)	6.0 (9.7)
10:30 (6:31)	2.9 (4.6)	5.7 (9.2)
11:00 (6:50)	2.7 (4.3)	5.5 (8.9)
11:30 (7:08)	2.6 (4.2)	5.2 (8.4)
12:00 (7:26)	2.5 (4.0)	5.0 (8.0)

Lesson 41: How Fast?

Run slowly, but not too slowly. George Sheehan, MD, another doctor who promoted running, said, "If the pace is too slow, it does very little good. On the other hand, a too-fast pace is self-defeating."

"Comfortable" is the key word, said Sheehan. He told runners to "set your inner dial just below the discomfort zone, then stay there—easing off the pace whenever it starts to hurt or increasing it when it feels too easy." Sheehan insisted that the body knows, much more precisely than any stopwatch or training schedule can tell it, what proper pace is. (He later added that a heart-rate monitor could aid in reporting exactly what the body felt.)

The trick is to cooperate with pain as a friend instead of fighting it as an enemy. This ties in with the concept known in yoga as "playing the edge." Ian Jackson, who popularized yogalike exercises for runners, recommended stretching carefully to the point of discomfort, backing off slightly, then holding that "edge" for a few seconds. The first sensation you notice is that the edge moves farther out without any excess strain. You notice after a few weeks of stretching this way that the edge of comfort has moved to a point you earlier could reach only with great pain.

"Playing the edge" also applies to the pace at which you run, said Jackson. It means finding that invisible line between comfort and discomfort. If you never nudge it, you never move it farther out—but if you push too hard, it breaks you.

If you want a more precise measurement, check your pulse while running. Proper pace for most training corresponds to approximately 75 percent of your maximum heart rate. Rules of thumb for determining the max (such as 220 minus your age) are imprecise, and pulse is difficult to take by hand. You must stop to take this count, which allows your heart rate to drop immediately. So if you want to check effort this way, invest in a heart-rate monitor.

As you advance in running, you'll learn to trust your body signals and instincts to set your pace. As you enter races, learn what your absolute fastest pace is for a given distance. Training typically is one to two minutes per mile slower (or an average of a minute per kilometer slower) than race pace for the same distance. An eight-minute miler (five minutes per kilometer), for instance, would do most of his or her running at about a 9-1/2-minute pace (or six minutes per kilometer). This will be slow enough, but not too slow—on the edge, but not over it.

The ideal pace for most runs—excluding speedwork and races—is one to two minutes per mile slower (or about 40 to 75 seconds per kilometer slower) than you would be capable of running all-out for a similar distance. Use a recent race time as your guide, or estimate your potential racing speed. Calculate that pace, then find your training range in table 6.2. The reverse is also true; you should be able to race an average of 1-1/2 minutes per mile *faster* (or a minute per kilometer faster) than you train at this distance.

Lesson 42: How Often?

Run at least every other day, but not *every* day. The training authorities generally agree on this point. Run three or four times a week, but allow at least one day a week off.

Table 6.2   Training Paces

Pace per mile (per km)	Fastest training pace (mile/km)	Slowest training pace (mile/km)
5:00 (3:06)	6:00 (3:44)	7:00 (4:20)
5:30 (3:25)	6:30 (4:02)	7:30 (4:39)
6:00 (3:44)	7:00 (4:20)	8:00 (4:58)
6:30 (4:02)	7:30 (4:39)	8:30 (5:17)
7:00 (4:20)	8:00 (4:58)	9:00 (5:35)
7:30 (4:39)	8:30 (5:17)	9:30 (5:53)
8:00 (4:58)	9:00 (5:35)	10:00 (6:12)
8:30 (5:17)	9:30 (5:53)	10:30 (6:31)
9:00 (5:35)	10:00 (6:12)	11:00 (6:50)
9:30 (5:53)	10:30 (6:31)	11:30 (7:08)
10:00 (6:12)	11:00 (6:50)	12:00 (7:26)

Bill Bowerman valued rest for all runners. "The well-conditioned runner learns early," he said, "that rest is as important to his or her success as exercise." Bowerman's major gift to training theory is the hard-easy system. Under it, his competing athletes took a hard workout one day, then eased off the next two or three before hitting another hard day. "In all my years of training national- and international-class runners," said Bowerman, "I have found that they progress more rapidly and painlessly by an alternating program of hard-easy. Chronic fatigue states are avoided."

For a new or returning runner, or one who simply wants to meet the minimum requirements of fitness, "easy" might mean a rest day—or at most a day when a related activity such as walking, bicycling, or swimming substitutes for the run. Kenneth Cooper's advice on frequency of fitness running remains the gospel: three to five days a week. Which means that two to four days are left over for doing something else, or for nothing but rest.

The competing runner who is older needs to give special attention to easy and rest days. Running times don't necessarily slow down with age, but recovery rates do. Bill Bowerman trained his college-age athletes by mixing hard and easy days. For the older runner, this might become hard day, easy *week*—with one or more of those easy days being the easiest of all: rest. The best day to schedule a rest is after the week's hardest session, whether long or fast—and especially after a race, which should be both long *and* fast. The longer and faster it is, the more you might need multiple rest days afterward.

Chapter 7
Rebuilding Program

Start running, walking, or both to repair your
fitness base that has eroded from neglect.

Lesson 43: Starting Overview

The first steps are the hardest to take. These are the ones that turn a nonrunner into a runner. Breaking resting inertia by getting up off the couch or out of the car and starting to reverse habits of longtime sitting is admirable because it is so difficult. Even if you have already started yourself, you can help beginners immensely by advising and applauding.

Everyone was once a runner, if only in childhood play. So almost everyone can become a runner again. How long it takes to reclaim fitness depends on how much time was spent slipping out of shape and how much weight was accumulated in the meantime.

Returnees to running come in two types—those who have never tried a formal program, and those who once trained to run but have let their fitness lapse. New runners have it tougher because they need to learn the rules of this game for the first time. But they aren't cursed with the lapsed runners' memories of times and distances they could run before but no longer can.

You can help these rebuilding runners by giving assurances. Start by helping them to celebrate small victories. Running a mile, or a kilometer, or even a minute can be an accomplishment at this stage, and anything runners do now is a long step forward from their recent inactivity. Tell these people that it's okay to split their runs into short segments with walks between. This isn't cheating, but rather a time-honored approach called interval training. Promise these runners that in the early months they'll make their greatest strides in the shortest time. Because of this, their first steps are not only the hardest but the most gratifying.

Lesson 44: Starting Lines

Congratulations! You have taken the longest step toward becoming a runner. That was deciding to start—or, more accurately, to start again, since everyone was a runner once. Still, despite the well-publicized benefits and popularity of this activity, relatively few adults take that first step back into running. Those who have reached a certain age may admit that they should start exercising more. They may even promise they'll begin—tomorrow. This is the same tomorrow-that-never-comes when they'll start their diets, cut down on their smoking and alcohol, reduce the number of hours spent facing the television, or drive more slowly and safely.

Changing one's old ways means replacing a set of familiar and comfortable habits (in this case, a too-easy life) with a new and more active—but also unfamiliar and uncomfortable—set of actions. This is never easy. The hardest part of starting to run is replacing one type of inertia with another. You remember the laws of inertia: A body at rest tends to stay at rest, and a body in motion stays in motion. Those facts of physics apply to the physical act of running as well.

First, the mind resists the motion and needs to be convinced of the new activity's value. You already have leaped that mental barrier. You already have listed your reasons for trying running: losing weight and looking better, gaining more endurance and speed (perhaps even enough to enter races), conditioning for other sports, pursuing the elusive "runner's high."

Now you can concentrate on clearing the physical barriers. A body accustomed to rest doesn't instantly spring into motion. No matter how willing the mind is, the body resists the early movements in the new direction. Demanding too much of yourself too soon invites an early and disheartening end to your running experiment.

The first few weeks and months as a runner are both exciting and risky. This is when improvement can come most rapidly—or when you can be injured and discouraged most easily. Each step must be taken most carefully now.

Lesson 45: Early Assumptions

The first assumption is that you are not now and perhaps never have been a regular runner. This may be your first attempt at a formal running program, or you may be trying again after an earlier

One of the hardest parts of running can be overcoming years of inactivity, but if you stick with it you'll eventually reap the rewards.

unpleasant experience. Either way, you are bound to feel awkward at first—not at all like a child at play who takes superb fitness and free-flowing motion for granted. You must reclaim fitness before you can move with any semblance of unconscious grace, and you must pay attention to every step lest you stumble.

The second assumption is that you expect instant results and will try too hard to achieve them. You think you can lose 20 pounds (nearly 10 kilograms) the first month, run for an hour without stopping, and improve your mile time by a minute all at once. Adaptation to this demanding physical activity doesn't come that quickly. You must coax improvement from yourself little by little with moderate but regular efforts and not try to beat yourself into shape. Overeagerness rarely produces instant success but often leads to frustration and injury.

Assumption three is that much of what you think you know about training techniques is wrong. Volumes of running "wisdom" in general circulation have filtered down from competitors and their coaches. Training for racing—with its emphasis on pushing through barriers of time, distance, and pain—is a specialized skill having little to do with you and your first goal of learning to run comfortably. You have a great deal to learn about how to run, and even more about how *not* to do it. Lessons on the mistakes that runners make would fill volumes much larger than this one.

Running Commentary: Out and About

Norm Lumian is one of life's ultramarathoners. He has run since age 12 and is now in his 70s. Post-polio syndrome is gradually taking away the use of his legs. Anticipating his future, he follows an unusual routine of a run one day and a wheelchair session the next. No one I meet on the streets and trails of Eugene appears to enjoy mornings more, even after all his years of doing this.

Norm, a retired college professor, often calls to "grade" my columns and to "assign" new ones. He said recently, "Why don't you write sometime about the simple pleasure of getting outside for a run each day?" Suggestion taken, Prof.

A regular route of mine takes me along a creekside path. On one side is a botanical garden, on the other a fitness center. Side-by-side treadmills look out of the fitness center, through a floor-to-ceiling window, onto the creek and garden. Both treadmills are always occupied at the time I run past their users' window to the outside world.

The treadmillers might be more fit than I am (and surely are younger, better dressed, and better looking). But I think while looking in on them that there's far more to running than fitness, and they're missing almost everything but the workout. Running only for the exercise is like eating just to build up the jaw muscles or writing to strengthen the fingers.

The run that touched off this story came on a springtime morning. The chilly air still carried a bite of winter, reluctant to depart. But the day's dawning came early enough now to let me see what I passed through and not just trust it to be there. This morning exploded with the sights, sounds, and smells of the new season.

Treadmillers miss most of this. The climate and light inside their clubs never change. They hear the grinding of their machines, or the background sound of music and news. They smell only each other and the deodorizers that mask the aromas of human effort. I applaud the treadmillers for their effort, which probably is greater than mine. But I wish they would step through the plate-glass window and experience the wider world of running outside.

Exercising indoors, and in place, is like watching the natural world pass by through a car window. You see it but don't feel it. You're apart from it, not really a part of it. In the gym, every day is much like every other. Outdoors, no day is quite like any other.

I'm out nearly every day of every week at seven o'clock in the morning. I run most of those days. But even when the day calls for a walk, I'm still out at the same hour, in the same clothes and on the same routes, for the same length of time. Boring? Never!

That's because no two days are quite alike. The Native Americans say you can't step in the same stream twice, and it's the same with days. Running days never exactly clone themselves. Conditions of weather, qualities of light, varieties of sight and sound are forever remixing into something new. Without stepping outside, you can't know exactly what freshness the day holds.

As you continue to run, you will begin to see improvements in how your cardiovascular system works.

Lesson 46: Aerobic Activity

When you become a runner, two dramatic changes begin to take place inside you. You train the aerobic mechanism, and you adapt to the stresses of running. The combined effects open the way to longer, faster, smoother running.

Running is essentially aerobic. Kenneth Cooper, MD, in his ground-breaking book *Aerobics,* defined this type of activity: "These exercises demand oxygen without producing an intolerable oxygen debt [such as sprinting does], so that they can be continued for long periods. They activate the training effect and start producing all those wonderful changes in your body. Your lungs begin processing more air and with less effort. Your heart grows stronger, pumping more blood with fewer strokes, the blood supply to your muscles improves, and your total blood volume increases. In short, you are improving your body's capacity to bring in oxygen and deliver it to the tissue cells, where it is combined with foodstuffs to produce energy. You are increasing your oxygen consumption and, consequently, your endurance capacity."

You know you're running aerobically if you can pass the so-called talk test. Try talking to a friend while running, or whistle if you're alone. If you can carry your end of the conversation or can mouth a tune, you're safely into the aerobic-exercise range.

The human body is an amazingly pliable instrument. It adapts to almost any activity it is asked to perform, balking only to protect itself from eventual destruction. The responses to physical activity are standard. Everyone reacts to exercise with the same general set of adjustments. Together, they're called the training effect.

The sudden jumps in ability that a new runner makes are measurable evidence of good changes happening inside. The resting pulse typically drops by 10 or more beats a minute in the first few months of regular running. The oxygen-uptake reading, a laboratory measure of the lungs' ability to take in and distribute this endurance fuel, improves by 10 percent or more. The blood pressure typically decreases by a similar amount. These and other changes in your internal chemistry and physiology add up to big improvements in performance rather quickly.

Cooper, who has analyzed the experiences of millions of beginning runners, wrote, "I like to think of the training effect as preventive medicine. It builds a bulwark in the body against most of the common cripplers. If you've started a little late, if one of the cripplers has already made its mark on you, the training effect can become curative medicine as well."

The first step a new or renewing runner must take is to clear away the effects of a sedentary life: Reduce the excess fat that has collected under the skin. Tone up the muscles. Inject more oxygen into the system. Strengthen and slow the heart. Correct degenerative problems if they haven't progressed too far.

Even when you start from what the physiologists call the deconditioned state, the changes are immediate and often dramatic. They follow Cooper's outline, and you can measure them easily by keeping three types of records: (1) running performances in terms of distance and pace, (2) pulse—not only resting but also while exercising—and the rate of its recovery, and (3) weight.

As training progresses, a runner should automatically go farther and faster with equal or even decreased effort. The heart pumps slower at rest, goes higher while causing less sense of distress, and returns to normal faster than before. Weight—if it was too high at the start—almost always drops, or at least fat weight is replaced by more useful and attractive muscle weight.

These changes come with time, and they can't be rushed. They arrive only at their own pace. By trying to push it, you succeed only in driving yourself lower on the fitness ladder. The same activity that builds up can also tear down if taken in improper doses.

This brings us again to the second key principle of running fitness: gradual adaptation to stress. You want to vaccinate yourself against the distressing aspects of this exercise. A vaccine is a small, carefully controlled dose of medicine. Taken in proper amounts, it sets up an immunity to a disease, but when taken in excess, the cure can be worse than the ailment.

In this case, aerobic unfitness is the disease and aerobic running the vaccine. You try to build an immunity to the stresses of running by running. When the doses are excessive, you overwhelm the system's ability to adapt and tear yourself down. But when the amounts are small and their increases carefully controlled, you grow stronger.

Lesson 47: Self-Analysis

Choose the number that best describes you under each of the 10 important health and fitness factors. Add up your total score to determine how to start training for running.

1. Cardiovascular health

3 = no history of heart or circulatory problems, including high blood pressure

2 = past ailments have been pronounced cured

1 = such problems exist, but medical care is not required

0 = under medical treatment for cardiovascular trouble (Warning: If you have such a disease history or are older than 35, enter a running program only after receiving clearance from your doctor—and then only with close supervision from a fitness instructor.)

2. Injuries

3 = no current injury problems that would affect running

2 = some pain during activity, but performance isn't affected significantly

1 = level of activity is limited by the injury

0 = able to tolerate very little strenuous work (Warning: If your injury is temporary, wait until it is cured before starting the program; if it is chronic, adjust the program to fit your limitations.)

3. Illnesses

3 = no current illnesses

2 = some problems during activity, but performance isn't affected significantly

1 = level of activity is limited by the illness

0 = able to tolerate very little activity (See warning under injuries.)

(continued)

(continued)

4. Most recent run

3 = went more than 15 continuous minutes

2 = completed 10 to 15 minutes nonstop

1 = ran 5 to 10 minutes

0 = able to run less than five minutes without stopping

5. Running background

3 = have trained for running within the last year

2 = no running training within the last one to two years

1 = no running training for more than two years

0 = have never trained formally for running

6. Related activities

3 = regularly participate in steady-paced, prolonged activities such as bicycling, hiking, swimming

2 = regularly practice vigorous stop-and-go sports such as tennis, basketball, soccer

1 = regularly participate in slow sports such as golf, baseball, football, strength-flexibility training

0 = not currently active in any regular sports or exercise programs

7. Age

3 = younger than 20

2 = 20 to 29

1 = 30 to 39

0 = 40 or older

8. Weight

3 = at ideal weight

2 = less than 10 pounds (five kilograms) above ideal weight

1 = 10 to 19 pounds (five to nine kilograms) above ideal weight

0 = 20 pounds or more (nine-plus kilograms) above ideal weight

9. Resting pulse rate

3 = below 60 beats per minute

2 = 60 to 69

1 = 70 to 79

0 = 80 or above

10. Smoking habits

3 = never have smoked regularly

2 = have been a regular smoker, but quit

1 = an occasional smoker

0 = a regular smoker

SCORES

A total score of 20 or higher indicates high fitness for a beginning or returning runner. You probably can handle continuous running for the prescribed periods in this chapter's program (see Lesson 48, page 86), and you might find that the early weeks of the program are too easy for you. Skip ahead if you wish.

A score in the 10 to 19 range indicates average fitness at this stage. You may need to take some walking breaks to complete the assigned runs.

A score of less than 10 shows below-average fitness. You might want to start with walking only, increasing the sessions to 30 minutes, before adding any running.

Lesson 48: Starting Plan

This is a three-month program for new and returning runners. Some of you can start higher than week one and skip some weeks, whereas others may need to repeat weeks. Use table 7.1 as a guide.

Directions: Schedule the running days as you please, but don't try to run more than two days in a row or to take more than one day off between runs. Fit the normal days' running into at least a half-hour session, walking the remaining time. Extend the run on the big day each week by 5 to 10 minutes—or an extra kilometer or mile. Run the scheduled amount all at once or in shorter intervals. Include some physical activity—such as walking, biking, or swimming—on the nonrun days.

Table 7.1 Getting Started

Week	Normal days	Big day
1	3 days of 10-minute runs	15 minutes
2	3 days of 10-minute runs	15-20 minutes
3	3 days of 10-minute runs	20 minutes
4	3 days of 15-minute runs	20 minutes
5	3 days of 15-minute runs	20-25 minutes
6	3 days of 15-minute runs	25 minutes
7	3 days of 20-minute runs	25 minutes
8	3 days of 20-minute runs	25-30 minutes
9	3 days of 20-minute runs	30 minutes
10	3 days of 25-minute runs	30 minutes
11	3 days of 25-minute runs	30-35 minutes
12	3 days of 25-minute runs	35 minutes
13	3 days of 30-minute runs	35 minutes

Lesson 49: Winner Inside

It is said that every fat person carries inside a thin person struggling to get out. Inside every new or renewing runner waits a winner about to surface. One hidden reward of this activity is an opportunity for any nonathlete to start winning right away and to keep winning indefinitely.

Time and distance let you win. No runner, not even an Olympic champion, can beat everyone all the time. No one can set the ultimate record that will never be broken. But every runner has the chance to go longer or faster today than he or she did yesterday.

You don't have to beat anyone to win. You don't have to reach any arbitrary standards of perfection, like finishing a marathon or breaking the five-minute mile. You win simply by improving your own standards, however humble those might seem at first. And never are your opportunities for improvement greater than at the start. Never will you gain so much, so quickly, from so little work.

The typical improvement curve in running climbs most steeply in the early months, when you can count on doubling your distance and dropping your pace by a minute per mile (or kilometer)—without a corresponding jump in effort. Improving like this is winning in the truest sense of the word: the personal sense.

Chapter 8
Fitness Program

Maintain your aerobic conditioning while
running less than two hours per week.

Lesson 50: Fitness Overview

One of the best movements in running history came from outside
the traditional activity. This was the birth of the swim-bike-run
triathlon in the late 1970s and its robust growth through the '80s.
Previously, runners had been monoathletes, indulging in no other
physical activity except their specialty—which they often took to
extremes. Few of them biked, swam, or even practiced strengthen-
ing and stretching exercises. They just ran.

The triathletes mixed and matched activities. They enjoyed better
all-around fitness than running specialists, along with better immunity to injury. The term cross-training was born along with the new
sport. Runners who still might not enter a triathlon or bike-run
duathlon now had permission to blend other sports with their main
one. They biked while recovering from injuries instead of trying to
run through them. They swam one day or two days a week instead
of running every day. They added exercises to stretch the legs that
running tightens and to strengthen the arms that running neglects.

Runners have learned that if well-rounded fitness is their goal,
running by itself won't achieve it. They need to complement it with
other aerobic activities and supplement it with strength and flexibility exercises. If your main reason for running is fitness maintenance,

then you start with this component. The FIT formula is simple: frequency—three to five days a week; intensity—a pace that's comfortable for you; time—20 to 30 minutes each of those days.

Round out the program by adding a few minutes of muscle exercises most days. Take a swim, a bike ride, a cross-country ski trek, or simply a walk on a day between runs or in place of an occasional run. Your body will thank you for the variety.

Lesson 51: Cooper's Prescription

The year 1968 was a watershed for personal fitness as well as global politics. As wars raged in Vietnam and on the streets of America, Kenneth Cooper, MD—then a physician with the air force—presented a radical message on the pages of a book called *Aerobics*. He urged readers to take to the streets in pursuit of fitness. We were suffering for our inactivity, he wrote.

Running is the most efficient way to train aerobically, said Cooper in that book. A brief run gives the greatest rewards per minute of time invested, and he implied that the more running a person did, the fitter he or she would become.

Looking back many years later on the first running boom that he helped inspire, Cooper observed that he made a mistake in not putting a limit on running amounts. He said that we runners (he was one of us himself) might stay healthier and fitter if we ran less. He wrote for the first time in his 1985 book *The Aerobics Program for Total Health and Well-Being*, "Recent research has shown that unless a person is training for marathons or other competitive events, it's best to limit running to around 12 to 15 miles [20 to 25 kilometers] per week. More than that will greatly increase the incidence of joint and bone injuries, and other ailments. On the other hand, less mileage will fail to achieve the desired improvement in the body."

Cooper and his staff at the Aerobics Center in Dallas were "overwhelmed" by research data showing the high incidence of injuries in people running more than 25 miles (40 kilometers) a week. Although a competitor might willingly take the risks associated with higher mileage, Cooper argued that running beyond his 15-mile weekly limit could yield at first diminishing fitness returns and eventually negative ones in the form of medical problems. For nonracers he set minimums and maximums: no less than two miles (three kilometers) three times a week, and no more than three miles (five kilometers) on five days.

John Duncan, Cooper's associate at the Aerobics Center, remarked that people running five three-milers a week "have the same low risk of developing heart disease as someone running 80 miles [130 kilometers] per week." Cooper agreed and added, "If you run more than 15 miles per week, you are running for something other than fitness."

Of course, many of us run for very good reasons other than fitness. Fitness, as George Sheehan has said, "is a stage you pass through on the way to becoming an athlete." Three miles might be the upper limit for absolute safety. But it might also be the *lower* limit for race training—as well as for the relaxed, recreational running that attaches us firmly and permanently to the activity. Three miles or less, taken every other day as if it were a prescription item, will make you fit. Three miles and more, taken almost daily, will make you a complete runner.

If you want to shed a few pounds or prevent a heart attack in later life, observe the Cooper prescription. But if you want to sample all that running has to offer, you need to run more. Three miles is about where running quits being simply an exercise and becomes a sport, quits being something you do to tone your body and becomes a vehicle for exploring the limits of your abilities.

If you want to do some of this exploring, look realistically at the effort it requires and the toll it might take. Be aware that racing has nothing to do with fitness as Kenneth Cooper defines it; the efforts involved are too great. When you train to race, you are no longer running just to lose weight and keep your heart in shape (although those benefits still accrue). You're training primarily to immunize yourself against the stresses of the race so as not to be hurt too much by them.

Race training demands some hard running because racing is hard. You need to teach yourself to run farther and faster than is comfortable. If that interests you, we'll talk about how to do it in most of the remaining chapters. But if your interest is purely in fitness running, you never need to train more than two hours a week and never need to run outside of your comfort zone in either distance or speed.

You don't have to run a marathon to be fit. A fun run with a friend three times a week can help you achieve and maintain a good fitness level.

Lesson 52: Extra Exercises

"When a runner goes into training," said George Sheehan, the sport's best-known medical adviser, "three things can happen to the muscles, and two of them are bad." The good effect is that the muscles most directly involved in the running motion become more efficient at it. But two other effects can cause trouble. Sheehan identified them as shortening of the strengthened muscles with loss of flexibility, and weakness of the opposing, relatively unused muscles.

This doesn't happen all at once. You probably won't experience either of these problems in your early months of running. However, the effects are cumulative, and runners can become increasingly tight and out of muscular balance unless corrective action is taken. Running by itself doesn't lead to total fitness.

Some leg muscles grow superstrong while opposing ones don't develop so well—if at all. A runner's arms, shoulders, chest, back, and abdominal muscles, for instance, don't get much of a workout but basically just go along for the ride when you run. Lack of flexibility is also a notable problem for runners who've trained a long time. The sport tightens their back-of-leg muscles, exposing them to muscle and tendon strains that might not happen if they remain supple.

Ironically, some of the most highly conditioned distance runners are less likely than nonathletes to pass simple tests of strength and flexibility such as lifting a large portion of their body weight, doing a number of sit-ups, or bending over and touching the fingertips to the floor without bending the knees. These athletes need to widen their range of activities. Maybe we all do.

Running Commentary: Taking the Heat

Nearly 100 degrees F (about 37° C). Two hours to go. This wasn't a long run but a midlength drive in the heat of the day. I took it as anyone would—with the windows rolled up tight and the air-conditioning cranked up high. I didn't like traveling this way, so cut off from real outdoor air, but I needed to keep my clothes fresh and mind unscrambled for a talk at the Portland Marathon Clinic.

I'm of two minds about AC, which can also stand for artificial chill. It's the best and worst thing that ever happened to America's summers. It helps us work longer indoors during the day and sleep better at night, but it comes at the price of softening us to the heat.

The air conditioner hadn't yet arrived during my growing-up years in Iowa. Some movie theaters had primitive cooling systems, but no stores or cafés did. No house I lived in or car that carried me offered anything cooler than the air a fan or an open window could coax in from nature. I can't recall that the Iowa heat slowed us down much. In my early years I played outside all summer with my pals. We kicked off our shoes and stripped off our shirts as we spent those months on the streets and playgrounds.

Later I ran all summer. Some days I'd strip all the way down to shorts— still no shirt or shoes—and train barefoot on the golf course grass.

The roads forced me into shoes, but I wore little else. Nearly naked runners weren't a common sight in Iowa in the early 1960s. A cop once stopped me for questioning as I ran this way through a riverside park. He told me, "We've heard reports of a flasher who meets your description."

I ran in the midday heat then. Didn't know any better. Three o'clock in the afternoon had always been training time at school, and this continued through the heat of summer. Then came my move to the West Coast and eventually to Oregon. Nature provides the air-conditioning here most of the time, in the form of cooling breezes off the Pacific.

The summers in Oregon are a runner's dream, with highs averaging a dry 80 degrees F (26° C) and overnight lows a brisk 50 (10° C). I've found no better summer weather anywhere in my travels. Yet these conditions leave an Oregonian woefully unprepared for the rare blasts of heat here or elsewhere. Compounding the problem for me is my habit of running at seven o'clock in the morning, which makes it almost the coolest time of day. At this hour I see dozens of other runners on the streets and trails.

Another habit of mine is to drive past Eugene's favorite running path whenever I go out, just to see who's there. The hotter the day, the smaller the count of runners. When the temperature pokes above 90 degrees (32° C), the Amazon Trail empties. Runners apparently read and heed the weather warnings to "curtail strenuous outdoor activity" on days like this. After one brief hot spell, a letter to the editor showed up in the local newspaper. The writer charged coaches and parents with "child abuse" for making kids play ball games in this heat. This thinking is wrongheaded because kids adapt to whatever they're given, as do adults.

The human body has a great talent for adaptation. Expose it to trying conditions and it builds immunity to them. This is known as the training effect, one definition of which is "use it or lose it." Hiding from the heat leaves you untrained for it. I'm trained to run only during 50- to 60-degree (10 to 15° C) summer mornings but do poorly outside of that narrow range. Put me in a summertime race in Kansas City and watch me sweat and suffer.

The more you bask in air-conditioned comfort, the less you can take the heat. Think of it as the training effect in reverse.

Lesson 53: Balancing Acts

To understand the benefits of supplementary exercises, you first need to know what they are not. They are not directly related to performance, and they are not the best way to warm up. You improve as a runner by training better at running, not by lifting weights like a shot-putter. You warm up best for running by walking and then running slowly for the first 10 minutes or more, not by stretching for hours like a yogi.

So why, you might ask, should you think about strength and flexibility exercises at all? In a word, *balance*—achieving a measure of parity between strength and flexibility, and between the development of the lower body, which works the hardest, and the upper part, which coasts.

• **Strength exercises**. Running itself is a form of weight training, since you lift your body weight about 1,500 times per mile. The legs, therefore, don't require much additional attention. But running's effects on the upper body are nil, so if you don't want to end up with the sticklike arms and the stomach muscles of a plucked chicken, you need to adopt the habit of regular strength building.

Choose simple exercises you can do at home without having to find a gym, buy expensive equipment, or use time that would be better spent running. A few minutes will give attention to the half of the body that running ignores. The simplest exercises are old-fashioned push-ups and sit-ups, and these are still quite effective. Daily sets of standard push-ups and bent-leg sit-ups, whatever number you can tolerate, will keep you respectably strong. If you want advanced development, move into more exotic exercises and sessions with weights.

A final note on another type of balance having to do with injury prevention: Since the front-of-leg muscles don't develop during running as much as the back-of-leg muscles do, pains in the shins and knees may set in. A simple way to strengthen these muscles is to sit on a table with the legs dangling, hang a weight on the foot, and straighten the leg repeatedly. This helps the muscles from the knee up. For the lower leg, flex the ankle up and down with the weight hanging on the foot.

• **Stretching exercises**. A great advance in training theory has been the growing popularity of so-called static stretches. These involve moving slowly to a position at the point of discomfort, then holding that position for several seconds. Static stretches differ from traditional dynamic calisthenics in both style and effect. The movements in calisthenics are active, and they can actually exaggerate the tightening they are supposed to prevent. Static stretching gently loosens the muscles.

Stretching is meant to counteract the tightening effects of running and is therefore best practiced immediately *after* you finish a run, not before you start. The muscles respond best to stretching after they have been warmed. Again, choose exercises with practicalities in mind. Fit them into your cool-down activities. Find stretches that require no apparatus and don't ask you to lie down on the cold, wet, or rough ground. Five minutes a day will loosen you up from running.

A good stretch after running can help keep your muscles limber.

Lesson 54: Supplemental Sports

Not everyone is meant to be a lifelong, full-time runner, and there is no need to be one to stay fit. Mixing and matching sports can produce similar results as long as the exercises are aerobic and are applied regularly for adequate time periods. Kenneth Cooper, the aerobics pioneer, said, "The best exercises are running, swimming, cycling, walking, stationary running, handball, basketball, and squash—in just about that order."

Running is a quick and practical way to reach the quota of aerobic exercise recommended by Cooper. But there are other good approaches to the same goal. Along with the activities he listed previously, high marks go to cross-country skiing, snowshoeing, and running in water while wearing a flotation belt or vest.

Cooper's minimum standard for fitness is 30 aerobic points a week. A mile (1.6 kilometers) in 8 minutes counts as 5 points, and six of those miles equal 30 points weekly. (Pace counts on the Cooper scale; a 6-minute mile gains you 6 points and a 10-minute mile, 3 points.) The approximate equivalents of an 8-minute mile (5 points) for other exercises: swimming 600 yards (550 meters) in 15 minutes; bicycling three miles (five kilometers) in 20 minutes; walking three miles (five kilometers) in 40 minutes; running in place for 12-1/2 minutes; handball for 35 minutes.

A runner with a slight injury that is too tender to tolerate much pounding but not serious enough for crutches might bicycle his or her points. Another might substitute swimming or water running on a hot, humid afternoon. The aerobic benefits of cross-country skiing are almost identical to those of running, and gliding across the snow is more pleasant than plowing through it. Mix and match activities day to day or season to season. The body requires and comes to crave continuous activity, but it isn't too particular about the specific type.

Lesson 55: Aerobic Options

Kenneth Cooper prescribes for fitness runners a session of two to three miles (three to five kilometers). At 10 minutes per mile (6 minutes per kilometer) this totals a 20- to 30-minute exercise period.

Running isn't a requirement, however. You can substitute or supplement with other aerobic exercises. Table 8.1 lists their rough equivalents in terms of efforts and benefits, as adapted from Cooper's recommendations.

Note that bicycling, skating, swimming, and cross-country skiing match running minute for minute in terms of efficiency, provided effort levels are comparable. Walking takes about twice as much time to produce benefits similar to those of running. Active games include soccer, basketball, handball, and racquetball, and only the time spent in motion counts toward the total.

Table 8.1 Exercise Equivalents

Activity and distance (if applicable)	Time period equal to running 20 to 30 minutes
Running 2-3 miles (3-5 kilometers)	20 to 30 minutes
Bicycling 6-8 miles (10-13 kilometers)	20 to 30 minutes
Skating 6-8 miles (10-13 kilometers)	20 to 30 minutes
Swimming 900-1,200 yards (800-1,100 meters)	20 to 30 minutes
Cross-country skiing 2-3 miles (3-5 kilometers)	20 to 30 minutes
Running/walking 2-3 miles (3-5 kilometers)	30 to 45 minutes
Aerobic dancing	30 to 45 minutes
Rowing	30 to 45 minutes
Walking 2-3 miles (3-5 kilometers)	40 to 60 minutes
Active games	40 to 60 minutes

Chapter 9

Speed Program

Improve the pace of your runs as preliminary
training for future short-distance races.

Lesson 56: Speed Overview

Fitness running is an end point for many runners. A quick physical
tune-up is all they want from the activity. A 20- to 30-minute run
every other day is all they need. Running is purely their exercise.

But others see fitness running as their starting line—as an intro-
ductory or warm-up phase. They reach the point of running half
hours easily and think: I'm ready for graduation. Where do I go
from here?

Postgraduate running can extend the FIT formula in any of its
three ways: more frequent running, more intensity, or more time on
the road. Your focus for now is on the middle factor: how to run
faster. Your runs no longer challenge you as they once did, and you
want to add an element of competition by upping the pace. Or you're
facing your first race and want to be sure you're ready to handle the
pace of an organized 5K (3.1 miles). Or you've raced before but are
stuck at the same pace of your training runs and want to escape that
rut.

Whatever your reason for wanting to go faster, the advice is the
same: Add some speedwork, which by definition means working
harder but not brutally so. You don't require a track, you don't need

to adopt complex or lengthy interval workouts, and you certainly don't have to run fast all the time.

As little as one fast mile a week—run on a track if you have one handy, but any measured course will do—blends neatly into the program you already follow. This mile provides a stimulating change of pace, both literally and figuratively. It stimulates improvements in speed and lifts you out of the one-pace routine. The slowest runners who have done the least speedwork respond the quickest to this small amount of it.

Lesson 57: Faster Plan

Pick an organized fun run of five kilometers as your target, and give yourself a month to prepare for it with the program in table 9.1. If you're running about a half hour at a time—as prescribed in the Lesson 48 program (see page 86)—this distance is now routine for you, so the event will be a test of speed. Improve it by running a fast mile (or 1,600 meters) for three straight weekends. Try to run the first of these a minute per mile faster than you go on the other days, and aim to drop the time each week leading to the 5K. Add easier warm-up and cool-down running on these days.

Table 9.1 5K Fun Run Preparation

Week	Normal days	Big day
1	3-4 days of 30-minute runs	1 mile (1,600 meters)
2	3-4 days of 30-minute runs	1 mile (1,600 meters)
3	3-4 days of 30-minute runs	1 mile (1,600 meters)
4	3-4 days of 30-minute runs	5K fun run

Lesson 58: Upping Speed

The difference between running and racing is measured not only in terms of an entry form and the size of the crowd, but also by your effort and pace. You work harder in a race than in everyday runs because everyone around you is doing the same thing; the crowd pulls you along. If your work is paying off as it should, you run much faster than you would on daily runs by yourself.

The effort you put into your weekly workouts will pay off when you get ready to race.

Just as your ability to cover distances improves rapidly during the early stages of a running program, so will your racing talent make dramatic leaps forward as you train and race faster. Speed improves even more rapidly than endurance does, and on much smaller and less frequent dosages of training.

As a new racer you can break personal record after record while applying the speed just one day each week. This may take the form of an actual race, where you get an immediate payoff on your investment in effort and pace. But you probably need to supplement your racing schedule with the racelike training in which the big payoff is delayed until race day. Either way, one fast day each week is enough speedwork for all but the most serious athletes.

The best way to measure improvement is to test yourself at the same distance repeatedly. That race distance most likely will be five kilometers, since races of that length are contested most frequently. The reason for its popularity may be that it is just the right length for the largest number of runners. The 5K is no more than the daily training stint for most of us, which makes it short enough to be an attractive distance to try to race. Improving speed comes from technique learned through repetition, both in private rehearsals and on the public racing stage.

Running Commentary: Faster Ones

The mile was my first love. My earliest heroes were milers. The first autograph I chased down was Wes Santee's. Roger Bannister made me want to break the eight-minute mile after he first broke four. My first timed run was a mile, as was my first race. The mile was the shortest distance that let me succeed as a runner.

My love for the mile never waned, but my practice of it did. By the late 1980s I ran nothing fast and had become a one-pace wonder—a runner with one slow gear for training and racing, for 10Ks and marathons. One of the fastest runners I've ever known, Dick Buerkle, and one of the slowest I knew in that pre-run/walk era, Marlene Cimons, pointed the way to a simple change. Dick once held the world indoor record for the mile and made two Olympic teams in the 5,000. Marlene, a reporter for the *Los Angeles Times*, was a one-pace runner.

Dick knew all about speedwork. But he also was a rare runner at his level who knew how to talk to runners who weren't. He wrote a short piece of advice in *Runner's World* about improving speed for road racing. I've talked about it ever since as the 1-1-1 plan: *one* mile (or 1,600 meters), *one* minute faster than your everyday pace (which is the only gear for a one-pace wonder), *one* day a week.

Marlene read this advice and tried the 1-1-1. She was stuck at 52 minutes for 10K, an 8-1/2-minute pace. Her first attempt at a breakthrough mile of 7:30 felt awful. "My running around the track was an uncoordinated waddle," she reported. "My lungs burned."

This was good, I told her. You're supposed to feel this way while teaching yourself a new skill. The mile would get easier—and faster. It's one of the few places in life where you can do better without working harder, as the form smoothes out and the breathing eases.

After a month of weekly miles, Marlene ran another 10K race. Her time: 48:30, a personal best by 3-1/2 minutes—or improvement of more than half a minute a mile on an investment of just one fast mile a week.

My reinvestment started in the summer of 1988 when I reentered the mile as a racer of sorts. My hometown conducts a series of informal meets, each beginning with a mile. The first week the leaders lapped me, and the effort required to run my 6:15 hurt a lot. Knowing the pain would ease as my times improved, I ran the whole series of seven meets and dropped to 5:44. Total improvement for the summer: 31 seconds.

My last road race before the track meets had been four miles at a 7:15 pace. The first afterward was five miles at 6:50—a 25-second drop at a slightly longer distance and with no increase in effort. The experience convinced me to restore a timed mile to my routine, regularly and permanently.

Today's mile isn't a race. I never try to run it all-out but hold an honest, faster-than-normal pace that usually falls in the mid-sevens. That happens to be what I ran for my first timed mile at age 10, in response to Roger Bannister's first sub-four. Each new mile keeps an old love affair alive.

Lesson 59: Race Rehearsal

Test is a blanket term covering training runs beyond the ordinary. Tests can be either longer than normal or faster than normal—whatever gets you ready for the abnormal efforts of racing. These are dress rehearsals for racing, and by necessity they are hard work that prepares you for the even harder work of racing. Long tests mimic the distance of the race but at a slower pace. Fast tests prepare you for the race's full speed but cover only part of its distance.

Race preparation requires distance and speed training.

The long test at least matches the time (but not necessarily the distance) of the longest race you plan to run but is done a minute or two per mile slower (averaging about a minute per kilometer slower) than racing pace. For instance, as a 50-minute 10K runner you would test yourself by running at least 50 minutes but perhaps covering only about 8-1/2 kilometers (or 5-1/4 miles).

The fast test at least matches the pace of the shortest race you intend to enter but lasts no more than half the racing distance. Say your lower limit is 5K, which you race in 24 minutes. This is a 7:45 mile pace (or 4:48 per kilometer). You'd test at this pace but with a fast training run of no more than 2.5 kilometers (or 1-1/2 miles).

The idea, then, is to bring together the two factors—full distance at full speed—in the race, where it counts. The tests are race specific. They get you ready for a single race or a set of distances. Later in the book we discuss how to prepare specifically for the short distances (chapter 12 centers on the 5K and 10K), middle distances (chapter 13 focuses on the half marathon), and long distances (chapter 14 deals with the marathon).

For now your task is simple. You just want to increase your 5K pace noticeably. Later, you might try more sophisticated forms of testing. Here are two that key off the distance and pace of your everyday runs:

• Double time—up to twice your daily average time or distance at normal training pace. If you usually run up to a half hour's worth of 10-minute miles (6-minute kilometers), test for as long as one hour at that pace.

• Half fast—no more than half your daily average, at 1 to 2 minutes faster than normal training pace. If you usually run a half hour at a 10-minute-mile (6-minute-kilometer) pace, drop to 15 minutes at 8 to 9 minutes per mile (5 to 5-1/2 minutes per kilometer).

In both long and fast tests, consider exercising the interval option. Interval training allows you to run longer and faster than you otherwise could or would. Intervals can be particularly valuable when you're breaking into the higher ranges of distance and speed—say, more than double your normal training time or more than two minutes per mile (1-1/2 per kilometer) faster than your typical training pace.

• Extra-long tests. Taking walking breaks can as much as double your longest nonstop distance with little increase in effort. Example: The race ahead is a half marathon and the intended testing time is two hours. Run 10 minutes, call a 1-minute timeout to walk, and repeat throughout the allotted period.

• Extra-fast tests. Mixing fast portions with recovery walks, in classic interval-training fashion, allows you to run faster than you could in a straight run of the same distance. Example: Your upcoming race is a mile. Run a fast lap, then click off your watch while walking for a few minutes. Repeat until you've run four laps and have a cumulative time for the mile, not counting the breaks.

Look for a large race for your first competition. The energy of the crowd will help carry you along.

Lesson 60: First-Timer Tips

1. Choose a big road race—the bigger the better. That way you'll be assured of having the company of hundreds, if not thousands, of first-timers like you. The excitement of the crowd will carry you along.

2. Avoid track or cross-country races. These are small and serious, and the experience of running alone and getting in over your head might turn you away from racing forever.

3. Be part of this race, but don't *race* it. Run to finish this first time rather than to exert ultimate effort. Make this a break-in event and go for a record next time.

4. Run no farther than you have gone in training. If your training so far has peaked at 5K, make this your racing limit for now.

5. Do nothing new on race day. Wear the shoes and clothes that you know are comfortable, and eat (or don't eat) as you would before any run.

6. Go to the race with an experienced adviser. This sport is all new and a little frightening to you, and someone who has been there at least once before can steady you.

7. Start in the middle of the pack or farther back. The serious folks line up at the front and race away from the line very quickly, putting at risk anyone who gets in their way.

8. Start slowly (in fact, you'll have little choice in a crowded race). Let the overeager runners sprint away. Many of them will come back to you later, when it's much more fun to pass than to be passed.

9. Time yourself, since official times at these races are often inaccurate. Start your watch as you cross the starting line, not when the gun sounds. The seconds or minutes spent shuffling to the line shouldn't count against you.

10. Be nice. Some jostling is inevitable in big races, but the etiquette of the sport frowns upon zigzagging wildly through the human traffic, cutting sharply in front of runners, or elbowing your way to a better position.

Lesson 61: Race Etiquette

Road races are popular and growing more so each year. And no races are better attended than those at the shortest standard racing distance, five kilometers. Fields in the thousands are common, and some draw more than 10,000 runners. Whenever this many people come together for any reason, problems can result if they don't follow the rules. Here are some traditional rules of the road, well known to and widely followed by regular racers. Newcomers are expected to learn and observe these rules.

• **Before the race**. If you don't enter a race, don't run it. Don't be a bandit who steals services from runners who have paid for them. Don't start any race that you don't plan to finish. Take your partial-distance workout someplace else where you don't demean the full efforts of others. Leave children and dogs on the sidelines. Baby joggers and leashed pets create hazards for the runners around you. Know what the pace-per-mile signs mean at the starting line (and it's not how fast you could run a single mile in your dreams, but what you expect to average for the full race distance), and take the proper position. Wear your race number on the front of your shirt or shorts. The back is for track meets. Never start in front of the starting line, blending in with the parade as it reaches you. Never start before the official gun, taking credit for a faster time than you earned.

• **During the race**. Run in a straight line whenever possible. Remember your high school geometry lesson about the shortest distance between two points. Look before you veer, and don't change lanes unless you're at least two steps in front of the nearest runner. Look also before you spit or blow your nose. If you take walk breaks, again, look behind you before stopping. Walk to the far right side on the road, ideally on the sidewalk or shoulder. Run side-by-side with no more than one companion. Don't create a multiperson roadblock for the runners behind you. Take out your own trash if you carried any bars or gels to consume along the way. (Drink cups aren't your responsibility, since the race supplied them.) Tell your spectator supporters to stay off the course. Instruct friends and family not to run out and hug you or run along with you.

- **After the race**. Run across the finish line, then keep walking through the chute while keeping your proper place in line. Don't exit through the side and mess up the results. Take only the amount of postrace food and drink that you can consume on the spot. Don't stock up as if shopping for free at the grocery store. Don't complain to the volunteers about the conduct of the event; they're only doing as they're told in a lowly and thankless job. Take your complaint to the race director—preferably in writing after the heat of race day has eased for both of you.

Lesson 62: Personal Records

To the runner, PR does not stand for public relations or an island in the Caribbean. It means personal record, and it may represent the greatest advance in the history of this sport. Running once picked its winners just as all other sports do. The first person to finish won, and everyone else lost. The winner—and only the winner—could add luster to a performance by setting a meet, state, national, or world record. The invention of the digital stopwatch worn on the wrist, however, turned each runner into a potential winner. Here was a personal yet objective way to measure success and progress. It depended not on beating anyone, but only on how the newest numbers on the watch compared with the old ones.

Be proud of your PR, but not so proud that you want to preserve it. Your records, like all records, are made to be broken. No one can break them for you, and no one else can take them from you. The PR is the only race prize that really means anything. Certificates and T-shirts are awarded to anyone who pays an entry fee, but records must be earned. They don't come to you automatically; they must be won in a race against the clock and against your former self. You win the race against time the way all athletes do: by preparing well then racing wisely.

You've done the training, you've run your break-in races. Now what can you add to your bag of competitive tricks that will shave extra seconds from the face of that digital watch?

- **Pick good races**. Race most seriously in the spring or fall, when the weather is likely to be most favorable for fast times (experienced runners prefer temperatures in the 50s Fahrenheit, or around 10° C). Choose a flat course designated as certified, which indicates that it has passed stringent measurement tests and is certain not to be long or short.

• **Avoid crowds**. For best results find a race numbering 100 or fewer runners per kilometer (maximum of 500 in a 5K; up to about 4,000 in a marathon, where runners have more distance to spread out). Massive races are human traffic jams that cost you valuable time, whereas smaller events allow you to start running at the gun and follow a straight course.

• **Compete**. Realize that your placing ultimately means nothing, but still use the people in front of you as moving targets. After the starting rush is over and runners up ahead have settled into their pace, reel in one "victim" after another.

• **Cut corners**. Don't run as if you were driving, always staying in the right-hand lane and making proper turns. Race courses are measured along the shortest possible route that a runner could travel, and you penalize yourself by straying from that path.

Chapter 10

Distance Program

Increase the length of your runs as a
step toward future long-distance racing.

Lesson 63: Distance Overview

Speed is finite. You can improve it a great deal, to be sure, and can keep going faster for a decade or so no matter what your age when you start running. But speed eventually plateaus and can climb no higher. If you run for enough years, you'll reach a point where your pace goes downhill.

Distance, however, is almost limitless. No matter what your level of talent, no matter how many years you have run, no matter how old your personal records are, the possibility of covering long distances still exists. This helps explain the appeal of the marathon. First-year runners can take pride in finishing one in twice the time the leaders take to finish, and longtime runners can feel good about going the distance an hour slower than their PR.

Not all runners can go faster, but just about anyone can run longer. It's a matter not of talent, but only of pacing, patience, and persistence.

The possibilities of covering distance have expanded greatly in recent years, thanks to changes in attitude and approach. The marathon spawned both changes. It welcomed a wider range of entrants than ever before, embracing not only running purists but also those who didn't mind mixing in some walking if that's what they needed to finish. Finishing times went up from earlier cutoffs around four hours to five, six, or more.

"Walk" ceased to be a four-letter word and became an accepted technique in extending distances. Taking walk breaks, early and often, brought longer distances within the reach of more people. A marathon, for instance, became less imposing when thought of not as a 26-mile or 42-kilometer chunk of distance but as a long series of 10-minute interval runs with pauses between them. You don't need to be a marathoner to use this trick. It works at any longer-than-normal distance.

Lesson 64: Adding Distance

Here we introduce you to the marathon, but only briefly. If you're just starting to look past a basic running program of the half-hour-a-day variety, we recommend against jumping immediately into training for the 26-mile (42-kilometer) distance. But you can take inspiration and instruction from the marathoners as you up your distance.

Despite a certain devaluation of mileage that has occurred during the running boom, the marathon remains the Mount Everest of the sport—a peak that every runner dreams of scaling at least once. If you haven't already gone to the top, that mountain is a more accessible climb than you might think. If you can race a 10K (6.2 miles), with a few more months' training you can tack on the additional 20 miles (32 kilometers).

This no longer sounds far-fetched. But it did in the 1970s when two physicians from Honolulu, Jack Scaff and John Wagner, invented the marathon training clinic. The Honolulu marathon was then, and still is, one of the country's largest. Other marathons are larger, but the remarkable feature of Honolulu was the large number of first-timers. Most of them were graduates of the Marathon Clinic.

Starting in March, hundreds of would-be marathoners gathered each Sunday for running lessons and a training run. These weren't hardened veterans of the sport; the majority were new runners or novices who had never before run farther than 10K. The clinic boasted that 98 percent of the people who stuck with the program finished the Honolulu marathon.

This clinic continues today, and dozens of similar ones have started up in other areas. Most of the major marathons now offer programs of their own to develop their own runners. Many other groups follow the principles of Jeff Galloway, a former Olympian and a *Runner's World* magazine columnist. Newly popular are fundraising efforts such as Team in Training, which benefits leukemia research. Such groups provide coaching and group support in exchange for charitable donations.

Adding distance to your run can help prepare you for a marathon.

The training provided by these groups is much different than the training that long-distance runners traditionally undergo. These programs don't see how many miles or kilometers the runners can pack into a week, scheduling few if any days off. They don't demand a long run every weekend, or a semilong one in midweek. They don't place primary emphasis on how fast the race course is run. They don't even insist that people run every step of the way.

Instead, the new programs keep distance totals relatively low. They encourage taking days off. They typically schedule a long run only every second or third week. They emphasize finishing. They allow walking. You can apply all of these tricks to your distance program, whatever your current distance goal might be.

You can see the marathon possibilities for your not-too-distant future. But first, if you're now in the 30-minute-a-day mode, focus on doubling your longest distance. Work your way up to an hour of running and completion of a 10K race. Then you can start taking the additional steps toward the marathon (covered in more detail in chapter 14).

Running Commentary: Beginning to Break

My history in ultrarunning—events beyond the marathon distance—is as undistinguished as it is ancient. It includes, all from the early 1970s, one attempt at 100 miles (160 kilometers) and two aborted 50-mile races (80 kilometers). My longest finish was a 50K (31.1 miles), and that was during the Nixon presidency.

My memories of ultras are as good, though, as they are long. Having tried them, I'll always appreciate the effort involved. And I'll always thank an ultrarunner for teaching me to walk. Tom Osler gave all runners permission to take walking breaks, and showed us how, in his *Serious Runners Handbook*. I edited this book, but even earlier I had experimented with the technique of breaking a big distance into small pieces.

What convinced me that interval racing worked was a 1971 race in Rocklin, California. The distance was 100 miles, which was farther than I'd ever run in a *week*, and I now had just one day to finish it. I didn't finish but did cover 70 miles (112 kilometers). This not only would remain the longest run of my life but also contributed heavily to my biggest week. This ultra was on a Saturday, and the previous Sunday I'd run a marathon. Token runs on the days in between (I never skipped a day back then) boosted the week's total to 110 miles (176 kilometers), or 30 miles (48 kilometers) higher than any time before or since.

Back to the 70-mile day: I wasn't terribly tired—or sore—at that point. But I'd already been on the road for 14 hours, it was two o'clock in the morning, no one else was visible, and I didn't see much point in running more laps on the 2-1/2-mile (4 kilometer) road course. When I told the lap scorer of my impending dropout, he said, "What do you mean you're quitting? You only have 30 miles to go!" That 30 would have nearly matched my longest previous run. But even as this abbreviated 100 was a failure in one sense, it was an eye-popper in three ways:

1. Most obviously this was double my longest nonstop distance, plus another eight miles (13 kilometers). This longest run ever was also my first use of intentional resting along the way. (The term walk breaks doesn't work here, because these were full *stops* averaging about one minute for each mile (1.6 kilometer) run. I just milled around for a few minutes during these breaks, then started exactly where the running had left off.)

2. Recovery from these 70 miles was quicker than I'd ever experienced after conventional runs of less than half this distance. Lost sleep was more of a problem the next day than sore feet and legs.

3. My running pace had held up much better than it would have in a nonstop run. It averaged about 7:30 per mile (4:40 per kilometer), or less than a minute per mile slower (40 seconds per kilometer slower) than my marathon the week before.

This ultra experience made me a lasting believer in breaks. It led eventually, thanks to Tom Osler's influence, to the run-walks that I now promote and practice. I never tried to clear up the unfinished business of that 100-mile race. Marathons are my upper limit now, and I'm still putting the old lessons to work in these mini-ultras.

Lesson 65: 30-60 Formula

Here's a simple suggestion for fitting running frequently and fairly far into your routine: Run long but not too long—long enough to feel that you've accomplished something, but not so long that running becomes like a second job. Most days, 30 minutes will satisfy the first requirement, and 60 minutes is the dividing line between enough work and too much to run as a standard training amount. Stop short of a half hour only when you're injured, ill, or taking a planned rest day. Exceed an hour only when you're preparing specifically for a race lasting that long, and even then go that far no more often than once a week.

This 30-60 formula is based on a rationale that we'll examine in a moment. But first let's hear from the formula's detractors—the proponents of fitness who claim that even a half hour is too much to run daily, and the serious athletes who maintain that a steady diet of 30- to 60-minute runs is inadequate.

Followers of the Kenneth Cooper School of Limited Mileage argue that even lower figures may be excessive, particularly if practiced without at least two rest days each week. Running this far every day is an invitation to injury, they warn. However, runners schooled on high-mileage training scoff at the one-hour limit. After reading the 30-60 advice in a magazine article, one athlete wrote: "The suggested training schedule is unrealistic. While I agree that recovery days are necessary, I don't believe that one hard day per week is sufficient training." He asserted that most "good to very good" runners exceed an hour at least every other day.

The recommendations here fall between the extremes. Many runners—and nearly all who have graduated to running in races—want, need, and can handle regular runs of a half hour or more. Yet few of them can tolerate repeated runs of longer than an hour. To veteran runners, the modestly paced 30-minute runs become almost as easy as resting—and the more pleasant of the two alternatives. This running itself is a form of active recovery from hard work.

Extra-long and extra-fast training—and, of course, racing itself—are the hard work. Precisely for that reason, a number of easy runs must separate the hard ones. We don't recover overnight, and we delay our healing by trying to put in too much distance at the wrong time. One or at most two big days a week is enough stress for all but the youngest and strongest runners.

Ron Maughan, a British exercise physiologist and running writer, addressed the question of recovery rates from various amounts of running. Reviewing a Dutch study that used rats as subjects in assessing degrees of muscle damage, Maughan noted, "The exercise intensity was not severe and would correspond to a fairly moderate training session in [humans]." Results of the study indicated that 30-minute runs on a treadmill caused no visible problem, while 60-minute sessions produced significant signs of muscle damage. Healing began the third day after the trauma occurred and was complete a few days after that.

These experiments with laboratory rats lend scientific support to the arguments that hour-plus runs hurt and half hour runs don't, and that every day of hurting must be followed by many days of healing. It is important to note here that healing is not necessarily synonymous with resting (though rest days are important, as you'll see later in Lesson 67, page 118). What it does mean is that you avoid damaging yourself further while recovery is taking place.

Lesson 66: Walk Talk

Walking. It's a simple and noble act that receives too little respect and not enough practice from runners. Many refuse to believe that the word belongs in their vocabulary or the act in their program. They're wrong. Although many runners still equate walking with giving up and dropping out, many others have found it can work small miracles. Selective walks permit us to go longer and faster than we otherwise might—and with less pain and no great increase in effort.

Tom Osler, an early proponent of walking for runners, wrote in his *Serious Runner's Handbook* that any runner can immediately double his or her longest previous nonstop distance without doubling the effort. The trick, he wrote, was to split up the run with 5-minute walking breaks. After Osler's advice on walking appeared in a magazine article on marathon training that recommended a 25-minute run, 5-minute walk formula, a reader wrote with three questions: "(1) Is there anything particularly sacred about the mix of 25-5 during the longest training runs? (2) At what point, if ever, does one wean oneself from the walks? (3) If one's last long run before a marathon included regular walks, does this mean he or she should walk during the marathon?"

The editor prefaced his response by telling the reader to think of walking as "long-distance interval work," a more agreeable term to many runners than "walk." Interval training is a standard practice in this sport and others. The intent of intervals is to cut up a big chunk of work into smaller, more manageable bites. In this case the intervals allow you to cover more total mileage at a faster pace than you could with straight running. Then came answers to the reader's specific questions:

- The 25-5 formula isn't chiseled in stone. Experience taught Osler that the 5-minute break is long enough to provide some recovery but not so long that it has a stiffening effect. Your trials and errors may tell you otherwise. The frequency of these breaks depends on how often you think you need them. (In recent years the 1-minute break, taken at least every 10 minutes, has become almost standard among run-walkers training for and completing marathons.)

- Wean yourself away from the walks only when you can run comfortably the full time of your next race and can recover from the training effort quickly. (Many slower and light-training marathoners never reach this stage.)

- On long training days you rehearse the distance of the race while still not shouldering the race's full workload. Walk breaks—or intervals—ease that training load. Save the experience of full distance and full pace for race day, when if you prefer you can start with every intention of running every step. (Again, some run-walkers prefer not to abandon the practice that brought them this far.)

Lesson 67: Rest Days

If you run a substantial distance every day of the week, a growing number of voices that ring with authority tell you that you're headed for trouble.

- **Item:** We again march out Kenneth Cooper's admonition that anyone who runs more than 15 miles (25 kilometers) a week—and more than five days a week—does so at his or her risk.
- **Item:** A study from the University of Arizona implied that anyone who runs with an unusual degree of consistency and commitment displays unhealthy obsessive-compulsive tendencies.
- **Item:** Sports medicine authority Gabe Mirkin, MD, commented that running can be a "most dangerous exercise," and that "if you run every day, you're headed for disaster."

Taking a rest day occasionally will help reduce your risk of injury and help you get more out of your regular training.

- **Item:** Evidence from the country's leading exercise physiology laboratory at Ball State University showed that people who continue training immediately after a race take about twice as long to recover as those who rest completely for several days.

Most of you are past the stage of running purely for fitness, yet we must stay healthy if we are to keep running at all. The balance is tricky to maintain. Three miles (five kilometers) might be the upper limit for health maintenance, as Kenneth Cooper has said. But this amount might also be the lower limit for race training and for attaching ourselves firmly to the sport. The first 30 minutes of a run, said George Sheehan, is for your body, and the extra time is for your mind. The first part is a warm-up for the good part.

Three miles is the approximate point at which the exercise becomes a sport. And you take calculated risks in the name of sport. Just so you won't think you're being told to take foolhardy risks, remember Bill Bowerman's "hard-easy" concept. Alternating work with recovery is basic to any sensible running program. Each day of hard work must be followed by at least one and probably several easy days.

To George Sheehan the word easy meant total rest. He once thought he needed to train every day. To stay with that routine, he limited himself to about five miles (8 kilometers) daily. Any more than that and he was tired and sore all the time. Sheehan's racing performances leveled off, then began to slip. He was, above all, a racer and couldn't tolerate slowing down. So he tried taking a day off each week. He felt better, so he wondered, "Why not two days?" Feeling fresher yet, he dropped another training session to see what would happen—and then yet another.

What happened first on Sheehan's eventual three-day-a-week program was that he could run more during each of his workouts. He both doubled his average distance and increased the pace on what became his Tuesday and Thursday runs. The second effect was that his weekly races began to satisfy him again. At age 60 Sheehan ran his fastest marathon, 3:01, while training only 30 miles (less than 50 kilometers) a week. This is hard-easy running at its extreme.

If you can stand to wait 48 to 72 hours between runs, you possess an unusual degree of patience. The point here is not that you should rest more days than you run. It's that an occasional rest day isn't a penalty or a sign of weakness. It's an investment in longer, faster, better running on the days when you do run. The longer you run (and the older the runner is), the longer the recovery period afterward. The quickest way to recover is by resting.

Lesson 68: Farther Plan

Take aim at a 10-kilometer fun run and spend a month preparing for it. If you're averaging a half hour for your runs—as the program in Lesson 48 (page 86) recommends—this 6.2-mile distance is nearly twice as long as you're now going. Lengthen your runs for three straight weekends without worrying about the pace. Add walk breaks if needed, pausing for about a minute after each 5 to 10 minutes of running. Refer to table 10.1 to help you prepare.

Table 10.1   10K Fun Run Preparation

Week	Normal days	Big day
1	3-4 days of 30-minute runs	40 minutes
2	3-4 days of 30-minute runs	50 minutes
3	3-4 days of 30-minute runs	60 minutes
4	3-4 days of 30-minute runs	10K fun run

PART III
Training to Race

Why race? Several reasons. For one, it takes you out of your neighborhood, where your runs might have become drab and predictable. It also lifts you out of your comfort zone, into distances and places that yield a higher sense of accomplishment.

Chapter 11

Targeting Races

Plan which events to enter, how to train for
them, and what your tactics will be.

Lesson 69: Racing Overview

Why race? On the face of it, racing is hard work, and that can hurt.
This work adds little to your fitness and might subtract from it by
causing an injury. Running with other people watching can also be
embarrassing, and that too can hurt.

So, again, why race? Several reasons. For one, it takes you out of
your neighborhood where your runs might have become drab and
predictable. It also lifts you out of your comfort zone, where tests of
body and will are lacking. Rehearsing for the race takes you into
distances and paces that yield a higher sense of accomplishment.

The race itself puts you on the line—not just the starting line but
at the redline of your abilities, where you can push no harder without breaking. Racing puts your training and resolve to their final
test.

You don't take this test alone but do so in the company of hundreds or thousands of runners like you. You aren't competing with
them; you're cooperating. The competition isn't with others but with
the distance, the course, the conditions, and the voice inside that
pleads with you to ease off. Everyone else in the race is tested in the
same ways. You push, pull, and pace each other.

This results in better running than any of you could have done alone. You can run farther, faster, or both in a race than you could in training because the race day is magic. No one cheers you when you're running alone on your home course. No one hands you drinks or reads your splits. No one gives you a medal or T-shirt or snacks at the end. No one pats your sweaty back and says, "Good run." Once you've sampled the magic of race day, you no longer need to ask, "Why race?"

Lesson 70: Testing Everything

May all your race-day surprises be pleasant ones! The best surprise you can give yourself is to run farther or faster—or both—than you ever ran before, or at least than you did the last time. Yet even that type of result shouldn't be too surprising. After all, haven't you trained with that improvement in mind? You've rehearsed in advance the stresses of the race so they won't come as unpleasant shocks on race day. You've tested separately at the racing length and at race pace. Long tests (lasting the approximate length of your race but usually run at a slower pace) acquainted you with the feeling of covering the full distance. Fast tests (run at race pace but no more than half the distance) introduced you to the mechanics of moving at full speed. Now you're ready to bring the two factors together in the race itself.

But the subject of testing doesn't end with distance and pace. These dress rehearsals serve many other purposes, all designed to immunize the runner against rude surprises. Very little that happens to you on race day should be happening for the first time. Don't just simulate the race on your longest and fastest training runs. Mimic the whole day. Start the night before the event by eating and sleeping as you would if you were about to compete, and continue pretending you were racing until you refuel and rest afterward. Pay special attention to three areas:

• **When to test**. Most road races, for practical reasons of traffic and temperature, start in early to midmorning. The time of day might give you problems if you normally aren't fully awake until noon or if you don't generally run until sundown. You can't change the starting time, so a personal change is in order on test day. Unpleasant as this might be, get out of bed two hours earlier than usual and perhaps take a shower before running to aid in the waking-up process.

Morning runners face a different set of problems on those rare occasions when races are scheduled in the afternoon or evening. You aren't accustomed to waiting all day to run, you aren't used to planning your daytime activities around a run, and most of all you aren't adapted to the warmer temperatures of the afternoon. Delay your tests until the time of day the race will be run in order to experience all of these conditions and to find ways of coping with them.

• **What to wear**. The cardinal rule is nothing new on race day. This applies most specifically to the single most critical item of equipment, your shoes. The temptation is to run in lighter footwear, thinking that every milligram of weight shed converts into minutes and seconds saved. This may be true in theory. In fact, you're giving up protection while adding greatly to impact stress. Any gains in time might be canceled out by muscle soreness at best, injuries at worst. When adding distance, speed, or both, stick with the shoes you know you can trust. Save the experimentation for everyday training.

The "nothing new" rule applies to clothing as well. Dress for the test exactly as you would for a race. Underdress rather than overdress, keeping in mind that apparent temperatures automatically rise significantly when you start running. Feeling comfortable at the starting line means you'll soon feel too warm.

• **Where to test**. Familiarity breeds confidence. If you know what to expect from a race course, you're more confident that you can run it well. Test yourself on the course itself or on a reasonable facsimile thereof. Match the surface, terrain, and surroundings of race day as closely as possible. Familiarity also breeds competence.

Lesson 71: Final Hours

You wake up, stand on the forward edge of the day, and tell yourself it is a day like any other—24 hours long, with the same sunrise and sunset as always. You say these things to calm yourself, but it isn't working. You know that today is The Day, race day, day of anticipation and dread. You made yourself a promise about this day weeks or months ago. You counted down the days as you prepared for it. You'll bore your family and friends with stories of what you did today.

But what *will* you do today? You can't know until your race is run, so you wait . . . and wonder . . . and worry. You feel the urge to do something, anything, but you aren't sure what. Uneasiness leads to aimless motion, confusion, and mistakes. Because you don't want to waste motion today or make mistakes, you need a plan. Make it up before the big day arrives, and keep it simple enough so you follow it automatically in the final hours—a time when you aren't sure you can remember how to tie your shoes.

1. **Get up early**. You might jump right from bed into a run on other days, but you shouldn't race that way. You risk injury by racing while stiff or sore; you surely give away too much time. With most races scheduled in the morning, get up several hours before race time, even if it means beating the dawn. Take a walk and a shower to wake up and loosen up. You won't miss the lost hours in bed if it means saving some time in the race.

2. **Stay close to the bathroom**. Your plumbing is twice as busy as usual. This extra activity is a natural part of race day, so don't worry about the amount. Just make sure you have a place to dispose of it. You don't want to carry to the starting line anything that might want out as you race.

3. **Eating is optional**. Do whatever you normally do. If you typically run 8 to 12 hours after your last meal, race without eating that morning. If you're used to eating before running, take what you know you can tolerate. You should realize, though, that all you're doing is filling an empty place; you aren't getting much new energy this late.

4. **Drinking is essential**. Even on cool days, racers throw off liquids at a prodigious rate. This starts before the race. You might already be down a liter or so of liquid as you start. Fluid loss while running is inevitable, but you don't have to give it a head start. Drink your way to the starting line, making sure you replace much of what your nerves are flushing out. Take small amounts, often.

5. **Arrive early, if you're driving**. Know your route, find someone to take you, and allow plenty of time. If you must travel more than an hour on the day of the race, plan extra time after arrival to

shake out the kinks of the trip. Give yourself an hour beyond the time you need for signing in and warming up.

6. **Sign in early**. Part of being a racer is enduring frustrating waits as officials take care of paperwork. Do your waiting in line as soon as you can and as little as you must. Pick a time when crowds are small, get in the shortest line, then hurry away to a calmer place. (Many races now allow you to take care of this business before the big day, such as at a pre-race expo. This is the better time to sign in.)

7. **Sample the course**. Walk or just stand and look at small parts of it, but don't run on it today. Race day is too late for a complete

Knowing what to expect before you go to a race might help alleviate some of the pre-race jitters.

tour. Your confidence is shaky enough without exposing it to every kilometer and hill. Distances seem twice as long and climbs twice as steep now as they will when you race them, so save those experiences for later. Just know where the starting line is, and find out exactly how you come in at the end, when exhaustion may confuse you. Know where the time checkpoints and aid stations will be.

8. **Avoid the crowds**. Part of warming up for a race is simply thinking about it. You think best alone. If you have time before arriving and checking in, isolate yourself as much as possible and rest. When the active part of warming up begins, do it by yourself, too. Even if you don't want to be alone, others may. Respect their privacy.

9. **Start hot or stay cool**. The choice depends on the distance you race. The shorter and faster the event, the more you must run before it starts. The longer it is, the less preliminary running you need. Before a one-mile or 1,500-meter race, for instance, take what amounts to a normal day's run of a half hour, stop for a few minutes to walk and stretch, then take two or three brief accelerations to top racing speed. However, if the race is a marathon, stay cool. Take no warm-up. Start running—slowly—at the opening gun and use the first few miles to warm up. Starting cool helps you resist the urge most marathoners have to start too fast.

10. **Remember that a little fear is good for you**. It gets the adrenaline pumping, and that will allow you to race farther and faster than you could if you were perfectly calm.

Running Commentary: Just Rewards

Ask runners why they choose to enter a particular race, and the type of awards given will appear far down on the list of reasons. Or at least this isn't a big concern to any but the elite who compete for monetary prizes. Most of us look first at the location and tradition of the event, the size of the field, and the speed of the course. But if awards don't rank high among the reasons to run a race, they stand at or near the top among ways to remember it.

While writing today, I wear a shirt from the Royal Victoria marathon. Near my desk hangs a medal from the George Sheehan Classic of 1994.

In a box across the room sits a collection of race prizes, including a seashell necklace draped over my head at the 1992 Honolulu marathon. And, oh yes, upstairs in a drawer sit more T-shirts than I can count. I give old ones away when the drawer overflows, but their number is still impressive. Each shirt represents a race completed. The harder the race, the longer I keep the shirt that recalls this effort. Marathon shirts are always the last to go.

The T-shirt has come to be the most common way to reward runners in the United States. Often it is the only way. I don't recall exactly when this tradition started, but I do know that it is unlikely ever to end. A few runners complain that they already own too many T-shirts and don't need to pay for another. A few races offer a reduced entry fee for runners who don't choose to take a shirt. But the vast majority of American races award these shirts because runners demand them. The shirt is the runner's way of saying during later training runs or trips to the grocery store, "Look what I accomplished." Race sponsors like the shirts too because they're a highly visible and long-lasting form of advertising.

The T-shirt is here to stay. But the more creative events practice variations on this theme. Some step away from the usual short-sleeved shirt by offering long sleeves or singlets, or occasionally even a sweatshirt for winter running. Some shirts become works of art. *Runner's World* conducts a yearly contest for the best T-shirt designs. Runners have been known to sew their favorite shirts together to make quilts.

Few races dare operate without shirts. However, many also give additional awards. The Hospital Hill Run in Kansas City hands out running shorts. The Honolulu marathon presents its shell necklaces or pottery medals. The Okanagan International race awards half a medal to its half marathoners.

Most events give some type of medal or certificate to all finishers. A cherished medal of mine is the one from the Sheehan Classic, with a likeness of the late doctor-writer on one side and a saying of his on the other. I also have special fondness for the certificate from my first marathon, Boston 1967.

These awards come with the runners' entry fees. Other mementos may be purchased at race expos. These range from jackets and hats, to drinking mugs, to personal photos along the course or at the finish. They all help keep memories of the race alive. But souvenirs that can be bought never quite match the value of prizes that must be earned.

Lesson 72: Racing Distances

Nearly all road races now run by the metric system, so if you grew up under the mile system, you must learn to interpret these distances. Table 11.1 lists the standard events and their mileage equivalents. One kilometer is 1,000 meters or .62 mile. One mile is 1,609 meters or about 1.6 kilometers.

Table 11.1   Metric/Mile Equivalents

Metric distance races	Mile system equivalents
1,500 meters (1.5K)	.93 miles
3,000 meters (3K)	1.86 miles
5,000 meters (5K)	3.11 miles
8,000 meters (8K)	4.97 miles
10,000 meters (10K)	6.21 miles
12 kilometers	7.46 miles
15 kilometers	9.32 miles
20 kilometers	12.43 miles
half-marathon (21.1K)	13.11 miles
25 kilometers	15.54 miles
30 kilometers	18.64 miles
marathon (42.2K)	26.22 miles

Mile distance races	Metric equivalents
1 mile	1,609 meters (1.61K)
2 miles	3,218 meters (3.22K)
5 miles	8,045 meters (8.01K)
10 miles	16.09 kilometers
20 miles	32.18 kilometers

Lesson 73: Equal Times

You can predict fairly accurately what you'll run in a certain distance without having run it recently. You can base the prediction on races at different distances. Pace obviously slows as racing distance grows and speeds up as it shrinks. But how much of a slowdown or speedup is normal? A good rule of thumb is to multiply or divide by 2.1 for each doubling or halving of the distance. If you race a 5K in 20:00, for instance, you can expect to run a 10K in 42:00—and vice versa (assuming you've trained equally well for the two races).

For more exact estimates of race-time potential, use the recent race distance closest to the one you plan to run next (see table 11.2). Multiply the shorter-distance time by the factor indicated to project the longer-distance time. Divide the longer-distance time by the factor indicated to project the shorter-distance time. All factors are based on a typical slowdown in pace of 5 percent as the distance doubles.

Table 11.2   Race Time Predictions

Distances compared	Multiply or divide by
5K to 8K (or 5 miles)	1.66
5K to 10K	2.10
8K (or 5 miles) to 10K	1.28
5 miles (or 8K) to 10 miles	2.10
10K to 12K	1.22
10K to 15K	1.55
10K to 10 miles	1.66
10K to 20K	2.10
12K to 15K	1.42
15K to 10 miles	1.08
15K to 20K	1.36
15K to half-marathon	1.45
15K to 25K	1.74
10 miles to 20K	1.28

(continued)

Table 11.2 *(continued)*

Distances compared	Multiply or divide by
10 miles to half-marathon	1.35
10 miles to 25K	1.62
20K to half-marathon	1.06
20K to 25K	1.28
Half-marathon to 25K	1.20
Half-marathon to marathon	2.10
25K to 30K	1.22
25K to 20 miles	1.31
25K to marathon	1.76
30K to 20 miles	1.07
30K to marathon	1.45
20 miles to marathon	1.35

Lesson 74: Race Pace

Even if you've done everything right in training, you can cancel all that with as little as one wrong move on race day. The first and worst bad move is leaving the starting line too quickly. Crowd hysteria and your own raging nervous system conspire to send you into the race as if fired from a cannon.

Try to work against the forces of the crowd and your natural desires. Keep your head while runners around you are losing theirs. Pull back the mental reins at a time when the voice inside is shouting, "Faster!" Be cautious in your early pacing, erring on the side of too slow rather than too fast. Hold something in reserve for the late kilometers.

The time for going to the whip is after the halfway point. The time for restraint has passed by then, and you run the rest of the way with whatever energy you have left. Again, you go against the normal trend of the crowd, and the inner voice pleads, "Slower!" Hold your pace while others are losing control of theirs.

This is where you reward yourself for your early caution, by passing instead of being passed.

Pay special attention to your times at the midpoint and at the finish. Later, compare your first- and second-half splits. These will tell you how well you paced the race. If the first time was considerably faster, plan to start even more conservatively next time. If the second part was vastly superior, feel free to loosen the reins next time. A steady pace breaks your records, while an uneven pacing (especially a too-fast start) breaks your heart.

Chapter 12

Short-Distance Program

Prepare for your 5K and 10K races, plus 8K and 12K.

Lesson 75: 5-10 Overview

We used to call 10 kilometers the perfect race distance—the perfect 10, you might say. This was a generation ago when runners were fewer and trained more than they do now. They took the sport and themselves a little too seriously sometimes. In an era when serious runners logged 10K a day or more, this distance was about as short as anyone would race. And 5Ks weren't treated as races but as informal fun runs for the less prepared and less committed. They weren't worthy of a serious runner's efforts.

Fortunately our thinking and practices have changed. We've turned the 5K into an event equal in importance to the 10K, which it should be since they both trace their heritage back to the track 5,000 and 10,000 raced at the first modern Olympic games of 1896. We've modified our training to where half hour sessions satisfy most runners. New runners, looking to graduate from their fitness programs, need an entry-level event better suited to their background than the 10K. The 5K provides a nice fit, and new racers have swarmed to it. One of the most popular series, the women-oriented Race for the Cure, runs at this distance. The well-attended Chase Corporate Challenge for company teams covers a slightly longer 3-1/2 miles (5-1/2 kilometers).

Longtime racers also have come to recognize the beauties of the 5K. It serves as one of the best types of speedwork for races of twice this distance, drawing out efforts that would be impossible to give in a solo training session. And they can take the 5K seriously for its own sake, running it often because recovery comes quickly. Racing a 10K every weekend might be risky, but these runners shake off the effects of a 5K in half the time.

The 10K remains an attractive race. But the five is even more perfect for those who want to start racing or to begin racing faster.

Lesson 76: Speed Needs

Adding distance is a matter of persistence—simply running more of what you already run daily. Increasing speed is a matter of style, of applying techniques not normally used day by day. Running faster is a learned skill, and you learn by practicing regularly with what is unfortunately called speedwork.

This word gives the impression that speed in any form is painful and therefore distasteful. Doug Rennie thinks otherwise. Rennie is known not as a technical writer on the sport but as a columnist who writes travel pieces for *Runner's World.* But he once ran times of 32:45 for the 10K and 2:33 for the marathon as a master (age 40-plus). He penned some fine lines about the need for speed, rebutting the common excuses for not training fast.

- *I don't need it.* "Ever run a 10K race that felt like a 50-yard dash lasting 37 minutes?" asked Rennie. A runner drawn into an unusually fast pace, a minute or more per mile faster than the training rate, feels that he or she is sprinting all the way. A sprint lasting more than a few seconds is no fun.

- *My races are my speedwork.* "If you race every weekend flat-out, and if every race is short and fast, then maybe you can get by with little or no formal speedwork," said Rennie. "But how many can nod in affirmation to those ifs?" The races must be frequent and must mimic the pace of the shortest racing distance. Otherwise speed training of this pace and similar distance must fill these needs.

Speed training before you race can improve PRs in the real event.

• *I'll get injured.* "Running with your head and not just your legs greatly minimizes the risk of injury," Rennie noted. Racing fast without a proper speed background maximizes the risk of injury. Frequent training at race pace eases the shock of an abrupt transition from gently paced training to hard racing.

• *Speedwork hurts.* "True, but so does racing," wrote Rennie. "Speed sessions prepare both mind and body for the rigors endemic to flat-out racing." You most fear the unknown. Racing won't hurt as much if you know what to expect and have experienced it previously in training.

• *Running on the track is boring.* "Who says you have to run on a track?" Rennie asked. "The important thing is that you create [racelike] stress. How and where you do it doesn't really matter." The speed training should match racing conditions, most notably the setting—which is almost certainly the road. You need to rehearse at racing speed on the track only if you plan to race there.

Lesson 77: 5K Plan

You routinely run 5K and beyond in training. You've completed group 5Ks where the emphasis was more social than athletic and more on finishing than running fast. Now that you have a benchmark for this distance, you want to run faster. The quickest way to do that is by upping the pace one day a week.

This one-month program focuses on speed building at about half the 5K distance so you learn to handle its pace. You also extend the length of one weekly run to about double the race distance, to make the 5K seem shorter. On fast days, run at your projected 5K race pace. On long days, run at easy-day pace but longer.

Prerequisites: Complete the program in Lesson 48 (page 86) or its equivalent, and be able to run at least 30 minutes nonstop before beginning the following 5K program (table 12.1).

Table 12.1 Training for 5K

Week	Easy runs	Long run	Fast run
1	3-4 days of 30 minutes	4-5 miles (6-8K)	1.0-1.5 miles (1.5-2.5K)
2	3-4 days of 30 minutes	5-6 miles (8-10K)	1.0-1.5 miles (1.5-2.5K)
3	3-4 days of 30 minutes	4-5 miles (6-8K)	1.0-1.5 miles (1.5-2.5K)
4	3-4 days of 30 minutes	—	5K race (3.1 miles)

Lesson 78: 10K Plan

The monthlong 10K program resembles the one for 5K, but the distances naturally go up for a race twice as long. Again, mix over-and-unders—fast runs of about half the 10K distance and long ones about 1-1/2 times as far. By slightly modifying the lengths of long and fast runs, you can adapt this program to 8K and 12K races.

Prerequisites: Complete the 5K program in Lesson 77 or its equivalent, and be able to run at least a half hour nonstop before starting the 10K program in table 12.2.

Table 12.2   Training for 10K

Week	Easy runs	Long runs	Fast runs
1	3-4 days of 30 minutes	7-8 miles (10-13K)	2-3 miles (3-5K)
2	3-4 days of 30 minutes	8-10 miles (13-15K)	2-3 miles (3-5K)
3	3-4 days of 30 minutes	7-8 miles (10-13K)	2-3 miles (3-5K)
4	3-4 days of 30 minutes	—	10K race

Lesson 79: Warming Up

The hardest, least pleasant effort doesn't necessarily come at the end of a run but often at the start. Recall how you feel as you take your first steps each day. You're stiff, heavy, uncoordinated. You wonder if you've forgotten how to run and why you're bothering to relearn the technique. Is this how you want to start a race?

Now recall how you feel after 15 minutes have passed. Sweat is flowing as freely as your strides. The running has taken control of itself, and you're on automatic pilot. Your early doubts about how and why you run are gone. This is the way you want to feel at the starting line.

Spend 15 minutes warming up before a 5K or 10K race. A quarter of an hour is long enough to loosen up both the legs and the head, but not so long that you squander the energy reserves you'll be needing soon. Keep this time period constant for races of all distances and paces, but vary the routine somewhat as working conditions change.

For instance, when racing at short distances (those lasting less than an hour and run quite fast), add two more elements after the 15-minute run—a set of stretching exercises, and striding 100 meters, three to five times, at the pace of the race. Stretching and striding become options at longer distances (those taking longer than an hour to complete and more modest in pace). Take a separate 15-minute warm-up run before any faster-than-normal effort of this length. However, if your objective is distance and not speed—such as in a marathon—simply warm up during its early miles as you would on a daily run.

Today's ambitious runners typically err on the side of too much warm-up. You see them pacing the streets a half hour to an hour before a 10K race. This amount of pre-event warming serves no physical purpose. It's a symptom of adrenaline poisoning. Think of how you feel after a normal day's 30- to 60-minute run. Do you want to start your race feeling this way?

Add a set of stretches to your pre-race and post-race routines.

Today's runners are just as likely to cool down too little. You see them crossing the finish line, stumbling to a grassy area nearby, and immediately starting the postevent celebration. This is no way to start recovering. If the warm-up shifts gears between resting and hard work, the cool-down period is a necessary shift from racing to resting. Continued mild activity gradually slows down the racing metabolism and also acts as a massage to gently work out the soreness and fatigue generated by the earlier effort. The pattern and pace of recovery are set in the first few minutes after the race ends.

The best strategy is to keep moving. Walk for at least 15 minutes after the race ends. Some advisers will tell you to run easily, but walking will give the same benefits with much less effort—and you've already worked hard enough. Tom Osler, author of the *Serious Runner's Handbook*, recommended a brief walk immediately after finishing, then another stroll later that day. "The worst thing you can do," he said, "is stop immediately upon crossing the finish line and stand around talking to friends." The talk can wait for 15 minutes. The cool-down can't.

Running Commentary: Home Run

Dr. George Sheehan defined himself as a racer who ran as a means to prove and improve himself in competition with whoever else showed up that day and whatever the course threw at them. The best-selling author and much-loved columnist and speaker raced more than a thousand times in his second career that started at age 45 and ended in the last year of his life.

Sheehan felt most at home at 10 kilometers. He ventured out from it often, going down to a mile and up to a marathon, but the 10K best suited his temperament and training. It was long enough to test his endurance but short enough to exploit his native speed. (He was the first miler over 50 to break five minutes, running 4:47.) He liked to race often and could do it once or even twice every weekend in the 10K range. Between races he seldom trained more than an hour at a stretch, which suited him perfectly for races lasting 40 minutes or so.

He came in well under 40:00 well into his 60s. Then a diagnosis of prostate cancer sapped his speed but not his will to continue racing as best he could under these circumstances. The slowdown through 40, 45, 50 minutes and more taught Sheehan a lot about the sport.

One of his favorite races literally brought him home. The Asbury Park 10K passed near his house on the Jersey shore. "Running with the pack at Asbury Park was enlightening and inspiring," he wrote in his *Runner's World* column. "I had always written as a representative of the also-rans, but in truth I was always an elite runner—one of the winners. I rarely came home from a race without a trophy, and more often than not was a winner in my age group."

Sheehan discovered that it wasn't for lack of trying that the middle-to-back-of-the-packers ran there. "What I discovered at Asbury Park," he said, "was that they were all running at the fastest pace they could. The eight-minute milers, for example, were taking no prisoners. They were not—as I once suspected—lollygagging along, engaged in conversation about last night's pasta party. They may not have the maximum oxygen capacity of those averaging two or even three minutes a mile faster, but it was costing them the same effort."

The cancer took Sheehan's life at 74 but didn't deprive us of his spirit. It lives on through his writings and even more so at a race named for him. After he died, the Asbury Park 10K was renamed the George Sheehan Classic and moved to another hometown of his—Red Bank, New Jersey. Sheehan worked at a hospital in Red Bank and ran out its door to start his training runs. Runners in this race on his old training course could now follow in the footsteps of a giant, whether they knew him or not.

Here is a story that Sheehan would have loved telling on himself. As we moved toward the start of his race, one youngster turned to another and asked, "Who is this Sheehan guy, anyway?" That's like asking who was that Kennedy with his name on a New York City airport.

Sheehan would have laughed off this lapse in his fame. He would have felt honored that so many guests had come to his home to do what he had done so often: search for the perfect 10. We sought to do what he had long recommended to all runners: "Be your own hero."

Lesson 80: Time Predictions (5K to 12K)

Performance at one distance accurately predicts potential at another. Table 12.3 compares times for short road races. Find your most recent result in any of these popular racing distances, then read across to estimate your current ability in the other events. Times are rounded to the nearest five seconds. For more exact calculations, see the conversion factors in Lesson 73 (page 133).

Table 12.3	Comparing Times (5K to 12K)		
5K	**8K**	**10K**	**12K**
15:00	24:55	31:30	38:05
16:00	26:35	33:35	40:40
17:00	28:15	35:40	43:10
18:00	29:50	37:50	45:45
19:00	31:30	39:55	48:15
20:00	33:10	42:00	50:50
21:00	34:50	44:05	53:20
22:00	36:30	46:10	55:55
23:00	38:10	48:20	58:25
24:00	39:50	50:25	1:01:00
25:00	41:30	52:30	1:03:30
26:00	43:10	54:35	1:06:00
27:00	44:50	56:40	1:08:35
28:00	46:30	58:50	1:11:05
29:00	48:10	1:00:55	1:13:40
30:00	49:50	1:03:00	1:16:10

Lesson 81: Split Decisions

Arthur Lydiard, the coach who did more than any other to revolutionize running, outlined a principle of pacing the mile race that applies to an even greater degree as the racing distance increases. "In my opinion," declared the New Zealander, "the best way to get full benefit of ability in the mile is to go out with the attitude that it is a half-mile race and, as far as you are concerned, the time to start putting on the pressure is when the first half mile is behind you."

Lydiard wasn't talking so much about a slow start as a cautious one. "The ideal starting pace," he said, "is the pace you know you can maintain all the way." At first it will seem too easy. Later the same pace will feel nearly impossible to maintain.

The coach, whose athletes have won Olympic medals at 800 meters through the marathon, added, "The three and six miles [5K and 10K] are far more exacting than the mile, and the athlete has to exercise more caution. It is far easier to go too fast, too soon in the six-mile than in the mile." This advice is even more sound for races of marathon length. Here the runner must exercise even more self-control. Early pacing mistakes that would mean a slower finish in a 10K are likely to yield a nonfinish in a marathon.

Lydiard has referred to even-pace running as "the best way to get the best out of yourself." For our purposes even pace means that the closer the two halves are to equal in time, the more efficient the pacing has been. If you start faster than you finish, you lose considerably more speed in the last half than you gained in the first. However, it is also possible to drop so far behind even pace in the early stages that the lost time can never be made up.

The safety margin for pacing is about five seconds per mile (or three seconds per kilometer) on either side of even pace. For instance, a 50-minute 10K runner would want to run between 7:59 and 8:09 per mile (4:57 and 5:03 per kilometer). These figures haven't been pulled from the sky. A review of world records indicates that most of the splits fall within one or two seconds per mile (about one second per kilometer) of even pace, and none of them varies by as much as five seconds per mile. If this method applies to the fastest and finest-conditioned runners in the world, it is even more critical for those with less talent, less training, and less to gain from bold tactical gambles.

Lesson 82: 5K Pacing

Talking about even-pace running is easier than calculating it. The problem is that races in the United States combine two measurement systems. Although most events are run at metric distances, such as 5K, splits are often given at mile points, and pace is usually computed in per-mile terms.

Table 12.4 takes those practices into account. It lists even pace per mile as well as kilometers and the desired splits at both 1-1/2 miles and 2-1/2 kilometers (the approximate and exact halfway points). The ranges of times are based on even pace, plus or minus five seconds per mile (or three seconds per kilometer). Determine your probable final time, then plan to start no faster or slower than the paces indicated here (tables 12.4 and 12.5).

Table 12.4   Perfect 5K Pace

5K goal	Per mile (K)	1-1/2 miles	2-1/2 kilometers
15:00	4:50 (3:00)	7:08 to 7:23	7:22 to 7:37
16:00	5:10 (3:12)	7:37 to 7:52	7:52 to 8:07
17:00	5:29 (3:24)	8:06 to 8:21	8:22 to 8:37
18:00	5:48 (3:36)	8:35 to 8:50	8:52 to 9:07
19:00	6:08 (3:48)	9:04 to 9:19	9:22 to 9:37
20:00	6:27 (4:00)	9:33 to 9:48	9:52 to 10:07
21:00	6:46 (4:12)	10:02 to 10:17	10:22 to 10:37
22:00	7:06 (4:24)	10:31 to 10:46	10:52 to 11:07
23:00	7:25 (4:36)	11:00 to 11:15	11:22 to 11:37
24:00	7:45 (4:48)	11:30 to 11:45	11:52 to 12:07
25:00	8:04 (5:00)	11:59 to 12:14	12:22 to 12:37
26:00	8:23 (5:12)	12:29 to 12:44	12:52 to 13:07
27:00	8:42 (5:24)	12:58 to 13:13	13:22 to 13:37
28:00	9:02 (5:36)	13:28 to 13:43	13:52 to 14:07
29:00	9:21 (5:48)	13:57 to 14:12	14:22 to 14:37
30:00	9:40 (6:00)	14:26 to 14:41	14:52 to 15:07

Lesson 83: 10K Pacing

Table 12.5 has the same rationale as the earlier one for 5K racing—even-paced running is most efficient, and the halves are best run within five seconds per mile (three seconds per kilometer) of equal time. Here are the recommended pace ranges for the approximate and exact halfway points in a 10K. Three-mile and 5K times are rounded to the nearest five seconds.

Table 12.5 Perfect 10K Pace

10K goal	Per mile (K)	3 miles	5 kilometers
30:00	4:50 (3:00)	14:15 to 14:45	14:45 to 15:15
32:00	5:10 (3:12)	15:15 to 15:45	15:45 to 16:15
34:00	5:29 (3:24)	16:10 to 16:40	16:45 to 17:15
36:00	5:48 (3:36)	17:10 to 17:40	17:45 to 18:15
38:00	6:08 (3:48)	18:10 to 18:40	18:45 to 19:15
40:00	6:27 (4:00)	19:05 to 19:35	19:45 to 20:15
42:00	6:46 (4:12)	20:05 to 20:35	20:45 to 21:15
44:00	7:06 (4:24)	21:00 to 21:30	21:45 to 22:15
46:00	7:25 (4:36)	22:00 to 22:30	22:45 to 23:15
48:00	7:45 (4:48)	23:00 to 23:30	23:45 to 24:15
50:00	8:04 (5:00)	24:00 to 24:30	24:45 to 25:15
52:00	8:23 (5:12)	24:55 to 25:25	25:45 to 26:15
54:00	8:42 (5:24)	25:55 to 26:25	26:45 to 27:15
56:00	9:02 (5:36)	26:55 to 27:25	27:45 to 28:15
58:00	9:21 (5:48)	27:55 to 28:25	28:45 to 29:15
60:00	9:40 (6:00)	28:50 to 29:20	29:45 to 30:15

Chapter 13

Middle-Distance Program

Prepare for your half-marathon races, plus
others of 15K to 20K.

Lesson 84: Half-Marathon Overview

The half-marathon is a fine race with an unfortunate name. Let's
talk first about that name before getting to the event's pluses. Half-
marathon is a cheapening and misleading label. No other race is
known simply as a fraction of another, yet this one is made to sound
like a scale model of the real thing. In fact, it is half of a marathon
only in distance but not in time. You can't simply double your PR
for the 13.1-mile or 21.1-kilometer distance and say, "That's what I
should be able to run for the marathon." It doesn't work that way.
The half is a distinct event with its own training requirements. It can
be just as demanding, in its own way, as the marathon because the
pace goes up.

Another distinction between halves and marathons is how runners view them. For most of us the marathon isn't so much a race
as a survival test. The big aim there is to reach the finish line some-
how, no matter how long it takes. The half is a race for most of us—
the upper end of our racing range, maybe, but still a test in which
time matters. Simply covering the distance isn't enough, even
though the distance can be imposing. It's longer than we habitu-
ally run in training, but not long enough to take all morning to

complete, or to wipe us out for the rest of the day, or to require a month's R&R afterward.

As long as you understand all this, you can overlook the name. No one has yet proposed a better one or has sold runners on replacing this event with a 20K—an underdeveloped race that has yet to be renamed the "double 10K."

Lesson 85: Half Efforts

The purpose here is to sell you on the hidden beauties of the half-marathon. It's a perfectly lovely event if, again, you ignore its ugly name, resist thinking of it as a second-rate event, and reject the temptation to double its time to predict your marathon potential. Don't think, for instance, that if you ran your half-marathon in 1:45, you must now be ready for a 3:30 race at the full distance.

No one expects Wilson Kipketer to run two more laps at his world-record 800 pace for a 3:23 mile. Yet we sometimes fantasize that a runner should be able to maintain half-marathon pace for twice the distance. If that were possible, American half-marathon record holder Todd Williams would be a sub-2:01 marathoner instead of a 2:10-plus man. Joan Samuelson, who holds the U.S. women's mark in the half, would have long since become the first woman to break 2:20 instead of running the national record of 2:21:21 that has stood since 1985.

The typical conversion formula between the two distances for top runners is to double the half-marathon time and add at least 5 minutes to predict marathon capability. For the typical runner the added time is about 10 minutes. But here we're falling into the trap we wanted to avoid. We cheapen the half by comparing it to its much bigger sibling.

The beauty of the half-marathon—name aside—is that it's a unique event. It has its own special training, its own pacing requirements, and its own rewards. Don't sell it short just because it isn't as popular as the marathon, or the 5K, for that matter. That lack of popularity is one of the half's many attractions. Very few halves draw more than a few thousand runners, and smallness might become an attraction after you've fought your way through megarace mob scenes.

This distance—or, more to the point, this *range* of distances start-ing at 15 kilometers and taking between one and two hours to com-plete—is a little-tapped source of personal records. These middle distances also offer attractions that frequently remain unexplored. The most significant of these is that the races combine speed and distance better than either the shorter or the longer events. Short-distance training, centered on 5Ks and 10Ks, leans heavily toward speed, since almost anyone can and does cover these distances al-most daily but would not normally approach race pace. Marathon training is weighted toward distance work, since almost no one ha-bitually runs this far and speed is much less a concern than endur-ance. The half-marathon requires modest amounts of both elements.

The pace of a half marathon race is not so fast that it requires a great deal of special speedwork, as might the events of 12K and shorter. These short races themselves, taken regularly enough, can serve as all the speedwork you need for the half. On the other hand,

Once you've started to tackle distance running, consider trying a half-marathon.

the half-marathon is not so great that it demands extra-long training runs, as marathons do. Two hours is the most time you ever
need to invest, and you can finish a half-marathon in even less time.
This is a welcome change from spending most of a weekend morning running and the rest of that day semicomatose from the extreme
effort of the marathon rehearsal.

Even if you train moderately (averaging 30 to 45 minutes a day,
for instance, with longest training runs 1-1/2 to 2 hours), no wall is
likely to loom between you and a half marathon finish line. This is
truly a *race* and not simply a survival exercise. When you don't hit a
wall, you spend much less time recovering. Jack Scaff, MD, who
founded and still conducts the popular Honolulu marathon clinic,
said that crashing during a race is "an injury, and you need six weeks
to recover just as you do from any other injury." By emerging from
your half uninjured by wall-smashing, you can repeat this distance
or race another one as soon as two weeks later. That's a more attractive outcome than needing to postpone your next big effort until
next month or the one after that while letting yourself heal.

Running Commentary: Fill the Great Gap

Road racing is polarizing. And I don't mean the split between faster
and slower runners or even pure runners and run-walkers. The split I'm
talking about is race distances moving to very short or very long, with
little in between.

The fastest-growing events on the U.S. roads are 5Ks at the one pole
and marathons at the other. Fives are logical starting points for newbies
and speed workouts for vets. Marathons are glamorous survival tests
for all. Eight-kilometers, 10Ks, and 12Ks remain numerous and attractive. We can still find enough races of 15K to half marathon. But between the half and the full marathon lies . . . well, not much. This 13-mile
gap is the black hole of running.

It wasn't always so. During the peak of my racing mania in the 1970s,
the northern California calendar alone offered a 25K in Golden Gate
Park, a 15-mile in the Gold Country, a 20-mile in Sacramento and another 20 through the Coast Range, and a 30K and a 17-mile on the
Monterey Peninsula. I ran all of them, almost every year.

Most of these events are gone now, and this trend repeats itself across the country. The "gap" races are too hard to sell to runners who seem to prefer races much shorter or longer. The only nationally known races filling the great gap are the Old Kent Riverbank 25K in Grand Rapids, Michigan, and the 15-mile Charleston Distance Run in West Virginia.

I hadn't run a race in the great gap for more than 20 years. Then I had to go to Canada to fill the void at the Around the Bay 30K in Hamilton, Ontario. Many of the runners I met in Hamilton were using this race as training for a spring marathon. So was I, with Vancouver coming up five weeks later.

An old belief of mine is that the best training for racing *is* to race. You can't push as hard alone as you can with company on the course and drinks, splits, and cheers dealt out as you go. This is the most enjoyable way to train. To work this way, the race must resemble the one you're training for in distance and pace. When the great gap goes unfilled, we've lost an opportunity to train for a marathon with the support from a crowd and all the other racing amenities.

A half-marathon race isn't quite long enough to serve this purpose (as I learned the hard way from trying several times to make one great 13-mile leap up in distance). Starting a full marathon with plans to drop out after 15 or 20 miles (as I've done more than a few times) feels a little like failure as you stop while your running mates continue to the finish.

Memo to race directors: Bring back the gap-filler races—the 25 and 30Ks, the 15 and 20 miles. Memo to runners: Enter them. They're great preparation for longer races to come, and great places to stop before the full reality of marathoning sets in.

Lesson 86: Half-Marathon Plan

Although this program applies specifically to the half-marathon, it can be adapted to a range of middle-distance races—those between 15 kilometers and the half, and lasting between one and two hours for most runners. These races might be both farther and faster than your normal training efforts, so you must prepare for both the added distance and the increased speed.

Another reason that the half's name is misleading is that it could be at least twice as far as you have run before in a race—or even in training. It might be three or four times farther than your daily average. This puts a premium on distance training for this 13.1-mile (21.1-kilometer) event. The two-month program increases distances two ways: (1) by widening the range of easy runs from a standard half hour to between 30 and 60 minutes, and (2) by extending the long run to at least 10 miles (16 kilometers) and as much as a half-marathon. Note that short races are recommended as occasional speedwork.

Prerequisites: Complete the 10K program in Lesson 83 (page 148) or its equivalent, and be able to run at least one hour before starting the following half-marathon program. With slight modifications you can also use this plan for 15K, 10-mile, and 20K races. Use table 13.1 as a guide.

Table 13.1 Training for Half-Marathon

Week	Easy runs	Long run	Fast run
1	3-5 days of 30-60 minutes	8-10 miles (13-16K)	—
2	3-5 days of 30-60 minutes	—	5K or 10K race
3	3-5 days of 30-60 minutes	9-11 miles (15-18K)	—
4	3-5 days of 30-60 minutes	10-12 miles (16-20K)	—
5	3-5 days of 30-60 minutes	—	5K or 10K race
6	3-5 days of 30-60 minutes	10-13 miles (16-21K)	—
7	3-5 days of 30-60 minutes	—	—
8	3-5 days of 30 minutes	Half marathon	—

Lesson 87: All-Purpose Program

Another hidden beauty of the half-marathon is that hardly anyone seems to train seriously and specifically for this event. Even runners as talented as Joan Samuelson and Todd Williams set their American records while pointing for something else—Samuelson to win yet another marathon and Williams while training for the upcoming track season, where he would specialize in the 10,000.

Runners of lesser ability and ambition can be half marathoners without sacrificing their normal lives to the gods of speed or distance training. Preparation for a half fits so neatly into what they probably already run that they hardly need to break stride while getting ready for this type of race.

How much of the following describes you? Your typical daily run lasts at least 30 minutes but rarely more than an hour. Every week or two you take a long run of one to two hours. You race often, mostly in the short-distance range in events lasting less than an hour. These races are your primary or perhaps only speedwork.

Now let's measure these practices against the accepted requirements of training. The two basic needs (beyond running easily on the majority of days) are (1) regular runs at the pace of your shortest race but a lesser distance, and (2) regular runs at or near the distance of your longest race but at a slower pace. (Full distance and full pace mix only during the race.)

If you fit the profile of two paragraphs back, you typically don't train quite fast enough for the 5K or nearly long enough for the marathon. But your combination of practices suits you well for the half-marathon. Your short races give the speed you need, your long runs provide the necessary distance, and your everyday running allows plenty of recovery time between the harder sessions. If you train this way, you don't need to change much, if anything, to run a respectable half-marathon race. Don't make any serious attempt to "improve" your program or to peak for a certain half. You are already training properly for this race. (If you don't fit this profile, see the buildup program in Lesson 86, page 153.)

You also are training well for a rather wide range of other distances. A half-marathon program suits you well for stepping either up or down in racing distance. You might consider this program as the home base for all-purpose training.

Inspiration for this program comes from Bill Bowerman. The legendary University of Oregon coach taught, as almost everyone now knows and practices, that good results can come only from mixing hard and easy days. Bowerman's years of experimentation taught him that no runner improved without working hard some of the time, but also that no one improved without taking breaks between bouts of extreme effort.

A lesser-known Bowerman principle involves training by cycles longer than a week. A variation on Bowerman's theme takes hard-easy to the extreme of no more than one day of racing or race rehearsing per week as part of a three-week cycle: fast on the first weekend, long on the second, and easy on the third. This yields an

If your typical daily run is between 30 minutes and 1 hour, you're close to being able to run a half-marathon.

average of about one hard day in 10, which appears to be a productive yet safe ratio—not just for half-marathoners but for racers at all distances.

The general schedule described in this lesson targets frequent racers covering distances between 5 and 25 kilometers without specializing in any one of these races. (For advice on more specific preparation, see the half marathon table in Lesson 86 (page 153), plus the 5K and 10K in Lessons 77 and 78 and the marathon in Lesson 93 (pages 140, 141 and 166.) In the following program you run through three-week cycles. You can race two of these three weeks. If no race is available, substitute a training session of similar speed or length.

Rehearse for racing at the full pace of a short race, but no more than half the racing length. Rehearse at the full length of the long race but at a slower pace. Mix full pace and full distance only in the races. On the other days of the week, relax, recover, and rest. Thirty minutes is the suggested minimum run and one hour the maximum. Allow one rest day each week, and an extra one or more if you're unusually tired or sore.

- Weekend One—short-distance race (lasting no more than an hour), or a rehearsal run at the pace of your shortest race no more than half that distance
- Weekend Two—middle-distance race (lasting one to two hours), or a rehearsal run at a similar distance but at the pace of your easy-day runs or slightly slower
- Weekend Three—easy weekend with no fast or long running, and especially no racing

Lesson 88: Time Predictions (15K to Half-Marathon)

Race pace changes at a predictable rate from one distance to another (you multiply or divide by 2.1 for each doubling or halving of distance). Table 13.2 lists equivalent times for the most commonly run middle-distance races. Find your most recent time for one of the distances, then read across to find your potential at another. These conversions assume that you are equally trained for the two races

Table 13.2   Comparing Times (15K to Half-Marathon)

15K	10 miles	20K	Half-marathon
45:00	48:40	1:01:10	1:05:10
50:00	54:00	1:08:00	1:12:30
55:00	59:20	1:14:50	1:19:40
1:00:00	1:04:50	1:21:40	1:27:00
1:05:00	1:10:10	1:28:20	1:34:10
1:10:00	1:15:40	1:35:10	1:41:30
1:15:00	1:21:00	1:42:00	1:48:40
1:20:00	1:26:20	1:48:50	1:56:00
1:25:00	1:31:50	1:55:40	1:53:10
1:30:00	1:37:10	2:02:20	2:10:30
1:35:00	1:42:40	2:09:10	2:17:40
1:40:00	1:48:00	2:16:00	2:25:00

and that the courses have comparable difficulty. (To compare times from events outside of this range, see Table 11.2 in Lesson 73, page 133.) Times are rounded to the nearest 10 seconds.

Lesson 89: Half-Marathon Pacing

Your halfway time is a key indicator of pacing skills, but few half marathons post a timer at the 6.55-mile (10.55-kilometer) point. Table 13.3 takes that oversight into account by listing desired splits at the nearby 10K mark as well as at halfway. The ranges of times are based on even pace, minus or plus five seconds per mile (three seconds per kilometer). Pick your probable final time, then plan to start no faster or slower than the times indicated here. The 10K and halfway times are rounded to the nearest 10 seconds.

Table 13.3 Perfect Half-Marathon Pace

Half-marathon goal (per mile/K)	10K	Halfway (10.55K)
1:05 (4:58/3:04)	30:10 to 31:10	32:00 to 33:00
1:10 (5:21/3:19)	32:40 to 33:40	34:30 to 35:30
1:15 (5:44/3:33)	35:00 to 36:00	37:00 to 38:00
1:20 (6:06/3:47)	37:20 to 38:20	39:30 to 40:30
1:25 (6:29/4:02)	39:40 to 40:40	42:00 to 43:00
1:30 (6:52/4:16)	42:10 to 43:10	44:30 to 45:30
1:35 (7:15/4:30)	44:30 to 45:30	47:00 to 48:00
1:40 (7:38/4:44)	46:50 to 47:50	49:30 to 50:30
1:45 (8:01/4:58)	49:20 to 50:20	52:00 to 53:00
1:50 (8:24/5:12)	51:40 to 52:40	54:30 to 55:30
1:55 (8:47/5:27)	54:00 to 55:00	57:00 to 58:00
2:00 (9:09/5:41)	56:20 to 57:20	59:30 to 1:00:30
2:05 (9:32/5:55)	58:40 to 59:40	1:02:00 to 1:03:00
2:10 (9:55/6:10)	1:01:10 to 1:02:10	1:04:30 to 1:05:30
2:15 (10:18/6:24)	1:03:30 to 1:04:30	1:07:00 to 1:08:00
2:20 (10:41/6:38)	1:05:50 to 1:06:50	1:09:30 to 1:10:30
2:25 (11:04/6:52)	1:08:10 to 1:09:10	1:12:00 to 1:13:00
2:30 (11:27/7:06)	1:10:30 to 1:11:30	1:14:30 to 1:15:30

Chapter 14

Long-Distance Program

Prepare for your marathon races, plus
others of 25K to 20 miles.

Lesson 90: Marathon Overview

These days, every neighborhood, every office seems to have a marathoner. The number of finishers in American marathons each year now approaches half a million. This might give the impression that almost anyone could run this far and might suggest that doing so isn't really as big an accomplishment as it was once thought.

These would be wrong impressions. Marathoners aren't one-in-a-million people anymore, but they still rank among the top two-tenths of a percent in the U.S. population for what they've done. The other 998 out of a thousand Americans couldn't or wouldn't finish a marathon.

The test is as big as it ever was, no matter how many people pass it. The distance is still the same as when it settled at 26.2 miles or 42.2 kilometers nearly a century ago. Running that distance fast is difficult, but taking two or more times longer than the leaders has its own challenges.

There is no easy way to get from one end of a marathon to the other—whether a participant is racing, running nonstop, run-walking, walk-running, or walking all the way. You can't just wake up one morning and decide it's your day for a marathon, as you might with a 5K or 10K where minimal training will at least let you go the distance. You must train for months before a marathon, often lean-ing on a group for support in the long runs. At the starting line of a short race you know you'll finish and wonder only how long it will take. You don't start marathons with the same confidence of reach-ing the end.

The long buildup to the marathon, the pre-race doubts, and the difficulty of the race itself aren't negatives. They all add to the attraction and ultimate satisfaction that you share with only one other person in a thousand.

Lesson 91: Galloway's Way

Jeff Galloway is a revolutionary. He, more than any other teacher or preacher of the 1980s and '90s, brought the marathon within the reach of thousands of runners who wouldn't or couldn't have got-ten to and through the event the old ways. To appreciate the value of the Galloway marathon program, you first must know the quali-ties of Galloway, the marathoner and the man. He has viewed run-ning from every angle—as an Olympian (on the track rather than the road), a sub-2:15 marathoner when that time was still a rarity for Americans, a running-store owner, a running-clinic speaker, a run-ning-camp operator, a magazine columnist and book author, and a leader of marathon-training groups.

Galloway ran his first marathon at age 18. He recalled that "weekly mileage of 30 [50 kilometers] barely prepared me. But I was falsely consoled by the thought that others in the race were worse prepared than I. The first 10 miles [16 kilometers] felt great. By 15 [24 kilome-ters], the distance of my longest previous run, I was tired. At 21 [33 kilometers] I was so tired I couldn't logically recognize that I should quit. Instinct kept me going, so I walked most of the last hour."

Logic could have driven Galloway into early retirement, but in-stead it sent him looking for better methods. He made the Olympic team in 1972 and nine years later, at age 35, he was still improving his times. More importantly, he had by then refined his training ideas to the point where he was ready to talk and write about them. He was a rare runner of elite class who knew how to advise the average participant in the sport.

Even then, in the 1980s, he spoke frequently to prospective marathoners. One exchange stuck in his mind: "I was giving a clinic on training. When someone asked about training for a marathon, I responded with the usual advice: Increase weekly mileage to 65 or 70 [105 to 110 kilometers], with a 20-miler [32 kilometers] each week for about four weeks. A non-'marathon-looking' person in the audience asked if one could run three miles a day and train for the marathon just by extending the long run to 24 miles [38 kilometers] or so. I said this didn't seem like enough training and that he might hurt himself on that sort of program. This fellow replied that he was currently using this program for his fifth marathon and hadn't been injured yet. I swallowed my 140-mile-a-week [225 kilometers] pride and asked him some questions."

The answers, and Galloway's later work with tens of thousands of new marathoners, led him to change totally his thinking about total training distance and length of long runs. He concluded that distance totaling is unimportant, if not outright dangerous, because it urges people to run too far on days when they should be relaxing. However, he also noted that he couldn't overemphasize the value of long training runs taken every two to three weeks.

"I'm convinced," he said, "that the greatest causes of injury are increasing total mileage too quickly and maintaining long mileage for too many weeks without rest." The Galloway marathon program, a masterpiece of simplicity and practicality, avoids both problems by mixing a few very long runs in among lots of short ones. It has three cornerstones:

1. A long run on alternate weekends at first and every third week at the high end, increasing by gentle steps from just above one's current peak to the total time that the marathon is expected to take.

2. Lots of filler between the big efforts, resting one or more days a week and running only three to five miles (five to eight kilometers) on the other days "to make sure you recover between long runs."

3. Walk breaks, averaging one minute each, taken early and often—a break in every kilometer to mile of running for most marathoners.

Galloway said, "I recommend this program, which avoids much of the risk of typical marathon training, while still giving excellent results. Thousands of three-mile-a-day [5-kilometer] runners have shown me they can finish the marathon without hitting any wall—much less the fortress I ran into. They added the one key ingredient I lacked—a long run gradually increasing to marathon distance. They also taught me the importance of easing up between long runs, and coming to the marathon eager and rested."

Lesson 92: Osler's Walks

Tom Osler was every bit the revolutionary that Jeff Galloway was, except that Osler's revolution came earlier and less publicly. His contribution, dating back to the 1970s, was the walk break. Osler didn't invent it, of course; mixing runs and walks is as old as human locomotion. But Osler legitimized it as a technique for running farther, easier, and safer in a long-distance event.

Osler was so heavy and slow as a young runner that his friends mocked him with the nickname Turtle. He was forced to make up with cunning for what he lacked in ability, and he was successful enough in this quest that he won several national long-distance championships.

As noted in Lesson 66 (page 117), Osler maintained that anyone can go right out today, without any special preparation, and double his or her longest nonstop distance. If you have run steadily for 10 kilometers, you can instantly make it 20. If your current high is an hour, you can last for two hours. If a half marathon is your best, you can complete a marathon. The trick, according to Osler, is to take walking breaks.

Wait a minute, you say, I've had to walk in my runs, and I can hardly start again. That's a different type of walking. It's walking because you *had* to, because exhaustion forced you to stop and energy and enthusiasm were gone. Osler's breaks aren't like that. You take them voluntarily, before you tire, as a means of stretching available resources.

This is a form of interval running. Osler's practice was to run 15, 20, or 25 minutes, then walk 5—perhaps drinking or stretching during the breathers. He followed this recipe in ultramarathons, races

You can go a greater distance if you add walking breaks to your long run.

well beyond the distance most of us run. Jeff Galloway and others have scaled down the Osler plan for marathoners by allowing shorter walks (typically a minute each) more often (at least once each mile).

The marathon plan outlined in Lesson 93 (page 166) combines the wisdom of Osler and of Galloway. It emphasizes the long run, allows an extended recovery period after each big effort, and includes the option of walking breaks if wanted or needed. Not everyone cares to take the Osler-inspired, Galloway-refined breaks. You might want to run every step of the way because pride dictates that you do so. Or you might walk during your long runs as a training tool and then trust the excitement of race day to eliminate the need for these breaks. Or you might keep using the refreshing pauses that brought you this far.

Lesson 93: Marathon Plan

Marathoners approach the distance with different goals. Some want to finish, some to improve their own time, some to qualify for Boston. The three-month program outlined in table 14.1 is flexible enough for all those purposes, allowing a fairly wide range of distance choices for runners of varying abilities and ambitions. Note the cycle of long run one week, half long the next (but at a some-

Table 14.1   Training for Marathon

Week	Easy runs	Long run	Fast run
1	3-5 days of 30-60 minutes	12-14 miles (19-22K)	—
2	3-5 days of 30-60 minutes	7-8 miles (11-13K)	—
3	3-5 days of 30-60 minutes	—	5K or 10K race
4	3-5 days of 30-60 minutes	14-16 miles (22-25K)	—
5	3-5 days of 30-60 minutes	8-9 miles (13-15K)	—
6	3-5 days of 30-60 minutes	—	5K or 10K race
7	3-5 days of 30-60 minutes	16-19 miles (25-30K)	—
8	3-5 days of 30-60 minutes	9-11 miles (15-18K)	—
9	3-5 days of 30-60 minutes	—	5K or 10K race
10	3-5 days of 30-60 minutes	18-22 miles (29-35K)	—
11	3-5 days of 30-60 minutes	9-11 miles (15-18K)	—
12	3-5 days of 30-60 minutes	—	—
13	3-5 days of 30 minutes	Marathon race	—

what brisker pace), and a short-distance race the third week. Note also that walk breaks are an option in long training runs as well as in the marathon itself.

Prerequisites: Complete the half marathon program in Lesson 86 (page 153) or its equivalent, and be able to run at least 1-1/2 hours before starting the following program. By modifying training distances, you can use this plan for races of 25K, 30K, and 20 miles.

Lesson 94: Time Predictions (25K to Marathon)

Here's how you can forecast times for the seldom-run long distances—those taking most runners more than two hours to complete. The times listed in table 14.2 have equal worth, based on the formula of multiplying or dividing by 2.1 as the distances are doubled or halved. Find the closest time of your most recent race, then read across for its equivalents. These conversions assume that you are equally trained for the races and that courses have similar difficulty. (Use table 11.2 in Lesson 73 on page 133 to compare times from events outside this range.) Times are rounded to the nearest half minute.

Table 14.2   Comparing Times (25K to Marathon)

25K	30K	20 miles	Marathon
1:20:00	1:37:30	1:45:00	2:21:00
1:25:00	1:43:30	1:51:30	2:29:30
1:30:00	1:50:00	1:58:00	2:38:30
1:35:00	1:56:00	2:04:30	2:47:00
1:40:00	2:02:00	2:11:00	2:56:00
1:45:00	2:08:00	2:17:30	3:05:00
1:50:00	2:14:00	2:24:00	3:13:30
1:55:00	2:20:30	2:30:30	3:22:30

(continued)

Table 14.2   (continued)

25K	30K	20 miles	Marathon
2:00:00	2:26:30	2:37:00	3:31:00
2:05:00	2:32:30	2:43:30	3:40:00
2:10:00	2:38:30	2:50:30	3:49:00
2:15:00	2:44:30	2:57:00	3:57:30
2:20:00	2:51:00	3:02:00	4:06:30
2:25:00	2:57:00	3:10:00	4:15:00
2:30:00	3:03:00	3:16:30	4:24:00
2:35:00	3:09:00	3:23:00	4:33:00
2:40:00	3:15:00	3:29:30	4:41:30
2:45:00	3:21:30	3:36:00	4:50:30
2:50:00	3:27:30	3:42:30	4:59:00
2:55:00	3:33:30	3:49:00	5:08:00
3:00:00	3:39:30	3:56:00	5:17:00

Lesson 95: First Marathon

Your first marathon is a graduation ceremony—an extended victory lap. The most demanding work, the buildup of distances that lasted for months, is behind you. If you have trained properly, you need not concern yourself too much with how the race will go; it is all but guaranteed to go well.

The wall that marathoners talk about shouldn't give you any nightmares. Oh, it is a very real part of this event, but not an inevitable part. Anyone, from the fastest to the slowest among us, can hit the wall, and anyone can avoid it. Those who crash have made mistakes, either in training or in pacing.

You will be well trained on marathon day if you follow a preparation plan similar to the one in Lesson 93 (page 166). Like a student cramming for a final exam, you may think you need to pack in all the work you can in the last week or two. Don't! You draw your ability to finish the marathon from a reservoir of fitness filled gradually over several months. Extra-hard work in the final days and weeks does nothing but drain the pool at the worst possible time.

Go into the race well rested. Allow three full weeks between the longest training run and the big event. Run minimum distances during the last week, and perhaps rest completely the final day or two. Save your trained-in strength for when it counts.

There isn't much else left to say about the marathon. The race almost runs itself. Just stay on course and keep alternating feet until you reach the end. You know by now how to choose a pace that will take you there, because you've rehearsed it many times in practice. Celebrate for the few hours of the race the good work you've done over the past few months.

Running Commentary: Days Like This

The T-shirt that I wore for this talk looked surprisingly new for one dating back to 1992. I'd pulled it from the drawer only on special occasions, and this day was extra-special. It marked my first return to Honolulu since I ran the marathon that earned the shirt.

My talk at Niketown last November began with the history of this red shirt. "I'm proud of it," I said, "because I took so long to get it." I joked about the Honolulu time being a PW—personal worst—but I didn't believe that for a minute. There are no bad marathons except those left incomplete. Some finishes just take longer than others. Mine have taken as little time as 2:49 and as much as 5:02. Like a father with 45 children, I can love each one, individual flaws and all. Each marathon is special in its own way.

I wasn't in Honolulu to run that city's marathon, but I told the audience there of my plans to run another one this winter. Two nominees, Cal International and then San Diego, came and went without me as work conflicts interfered. The backup to the backup race was Las Vegas. My wife, Barbara, and I aren't Vegas types, being too cheap to gamble and too straight to drink. But the February timing of the race was right, and the desert vacation afterward was appealing to us soggy and chilled Oregonians.

Anyone knowing my history of marathon times and counts might wonder, why bother? Why repeat what I've done dozens of times before, and take an extra hour or two to do it? Why not just skip the race and go right into the vacation? I don't ask myself any of this, and here's why. Days like this are too rare to miss. In the 15,000 days of my running life, marathons have occupied only 45 of them—or 0.3 percent of the total. These few days help fuel the many others, by giving higher goals and supplying greater memories.

I'll spare you a mile-by-mile account of my leisurely, walk-punctuated Sunday morning on the Old Los Angeles Highway, leading toward the high-rises of the Strip. It's enough to say that the day brought all the effort and elation, familiarity and surprises that marathon days always provide—and few others ever do.

Which meant that the marathon was well worth my time. All 4:25 of it. This time confers no bragging rights. It's nearly double that of the race's leader, someone I never saw and whose name I'm not moved to look up. We ran the same course but in different worlds that day.

The time was my second slowest, but *not* the second worst. I don't rank marathons that way anymore, because slower no longer means lesser. Each one has its own struggles and rewards.

Now I own a T-shirt from the Las Vegas Marathon. I'll wear it proudly, on special occasions only, while looking forward to the next day like this.

Lesson 96: Marathon Pacing

In no race is early caution more critical than in the marathon. The wall awaits those runners who start too fast. (Starting too slowly is seldom a problem with marathoners.) Table 14.3 lists the desired splits at the halfway point as well as at five-kilometer intervals. The ranges of times are based on even pace, minus or plus five seconds per mile (three seconds per kilometer). Realistically predict your final time, then plan to start no faster or slower than indicated here. The 5Ks are rounded to the nearest five seconds and half-marathons to the nearest minute.

Table 14.3   Perfect Marathon Pace

Marathon goal (per mile/K)	5K splits	Half marathon
2:20 (5:21/3:19)	16:25 to 16:40	1:09 to 1:11
2:30 (5:44/3:33)	17:40 to 17:55	1:14 to 1:16
2:40 (6:06/3:47)	18:50 to 19:05	1:19 to 1:21
2:50 (6:29/4:02)	20:00 to 20:15	1:24 to 1:26
3:00 (6:52/4:16)	21:10 to 21:25	1:29 to 1:31
3:10 (7:15/4:30)	22:25 to 22:40	1:34 to 1:36
3:20 (7:38/4:44)	23:35 to 23:50	1:39 to 1:41
3:30 (8:01/4:58)	24:45 to 25:00	1:44 to 1:46
3:40 (8:24/5:12)	25:55 to 26:10	1:49 to 1:51
3:50 (8:47/5:27)	27:05 to 27:20	1:54 to 1:56
4:00 (9:09/5:41)	28:20 to 28:35	1:59 to 2:01
4:10 (9:32/5:55)	29:30 to 29:45	2:04 to 2:06
4:20 (9:55/6:10)	30:40 to 30:55	2:09 to 2:11
4:30 (10:18/6:24)	31:50 to 32:15	2:14 to 2:16
4:40 (10:41/6:38)	33:00 to 33:15	2:19 to 2:21
4:50 (11:04/6:52)	34:15 to 34:30	2:24 to 2:26
5:00 (11:27/7:06)	35:25 to 35:40	2:29 to 2:31
5:10 (11:50/7:21)	36:35 to 36:50	2:34 to 2:36
5:20 (12:12/7:35)	37:45 to 38:00	2:39 to 2:41
5:30 (12:36/7:49)	39:00 to 39:15	2:44 to 2:46
5:40 (12:58/8:03)	40:10 to 40:25	2:49 to 2:51
5:50 (13:21/8:18)	41:20 to 41:35	2:54 to 2:56
6:00 (13:45/8:32)	42:30 to 42:45	2:59 to 3:01

Chapter 15

Race-Recovery Program

Ease back into training in the days and
weeks after your race.

Lesson 97: Recovery Overview

One of the most important phases of a training program is also one of the most overlooked. This is what to do *after* the race. It doesn't end at the finish line but continues with what you do—or don't do—in the immediate and extended period afterward.

Racing is motivating, challenging, and exciting. It also is demanding, difficult, and damaging. The magic of race day adds to your normal distances and increases your normal paces, but not without a price. Going past your limits one day requires that you repay that debt later by staying well below those limits. The longer the race, the larger the debt. You might get over a 5K race in a few days, but a marathon will take many weeks.

Recovery passes through stages. Think of them as the three Rs—resting, rebuilding, and refocusing. The quickest and surest therapy for acute post-race soreness and fatigue is a day or two or more of rest. You rebuild by returning to very easy runs—nothing long, nothing fast, and certainly no more races—and gradually working them back toward normal. You're ready to refocus on the next race only when the memory of the last one's difficulty fades and the excitement for harder work returns. Only then does long and fast training resume.

How long recovery takes will again depend on the length of the last race. One popular rule of thumb is to allow at least one easy day for every mile of the race. One day per kilometer (e.g., 10 days after a 10K to six weeks after a marathon) might work even better, especially for older runners. Race times don't necessarily slow with age, but recovery rates usually do.

Lesson 98: Clearing Damage

Racing is as destructive as it is exciting. Don't miss the excitement, but take extreme care in handling the destruction. Recover from the race as if it were an injury that takes time to heal.

The healing period starts or stalls immediately after you finish the race, depending on how you treat yourself right away. If you stop two steps past the line, stagger to the nearest grassy spot, and sit or lie there uncovered for the next hour, you'll recover slowly. The next few days' runs will feel like they've been added onto the end of your race—or worse. But if you keep moving and cool down slowly, the damage done by the race is erased sooner.

The post-race air feels instantly cooler by what seems like 20 degrees F (about $10°$ C). You cool it simply by stopping. That's why you need to put on more clothes than you wore to race. Change to a dry shirt even if the day is warm, jacket and pants if it's cool, and gloves and a cap if it's cold.

Resist the temptation to strip till you're next to naked or to jump right into a pool in warm weather, or to go right inside from the cold to a hot shower. Either choice invites injury or illness later. The body gets enough of a shock from racing, without being subjected to such drastic temperature changes. Reserves to fight off illness have already been depleted by the racing effort. You don't need much of an extra jolt to trigger a cold or a case of flu.

Something else is guaranteed if you don't keep moving. Your overworked muscles, saturated with fatigue products, stiffen quickly if you stop suddenly. They have less trouble if you slow them by degrees. Don't sit down immediately. Continue mild exercise in the form of walking or very easy running for the next 15 minutes or so.

What you do on race day merely begins the healing process. Soreness peaks the second day after a race, then disappears within a few more days. Yet a much deeper and more subtle weariness lingers for many days after a 5K race and many weeks after a marathon.

Racers (particularly those running the longest distances with extended recovery periods) who jump back into full training and racing before the healing is complete keep the sports medicine specialists busy. Limping into the clinic a week after the race, the runner complains, "I had no problems in the race, then this happened during yesterday's long run. What bad luck!" Luck had nothing to do with it. Heaping abuse on a battered body yielded this predictable result.

Running Commentary: Lessons from Layoffs

A long-lasting injury or illness can be good for a runner. By long, I mean weeks or even months, not days. The longer the layoff, the better the lessons about what running really means to you.

This isn't true at first, of course. Pain and suffering are never pleasant, and they don't allow philosophical insights to break through. All you want early in the ailment is for the hurting to stop. The worst of the pain might come not from the ailment itself but from not running and wondering if you ever will run again. During this stage you can't stand to see or talk to or read about healthy runners. They remind you too painfully of all that you are not. This stage eventually and inevitably passes. The pain settles down and then eases, and your head clears. You now see what went wrong.

Your illness or injury was no accident. You got what you paid for, or more likely the bill came due for not paying out enough in advance of your last big effort. Say you ran a marathon a few weeks ago. It was your first in years, and by most standards your training had fallen short of adequate. Your longest run before the marathon was 30 kilometers. This left you more than a mile shy of the 20 miles that most advisers on the subject call minimum premarathon distance. So you probably hadn't paid enough into your training account.

You ran the marathon anyway, trusting experience and the magic of race day to carry you through. They did, but it was a long and tough day, especially the final miles. The less training you've undergone, the more sporadic the racing, and the harder the effort, the longer the recovery time. A hard-training, regular racer might be immune to most of the stresses of racing and might bounce back from a marathon in a week or two.

A lightly trained, infrequent racer hasn't built such immunity. A marathon might require six or more truly easy weeks afterward. So what happens if you fit this description and try to resume normal running in fewer than the needed number of weeks? If you don't voluntarily take the full time needed for recovery, the body demands it from you as an injury or illness. Healing that problem then occupies the weeks when you would have been getting over the marathon anyway.

As you come out of the dark spell and begin to run again, you see that the troubles have helped you. They have shown you what means the most to you in your running. This is not finishing a marathon or taking the long runs that lead up to one. Nor is it shorter races or the fast training that prepares you for them. What you missed most was getting out for the little everyday runs, the fillers. They're the ones not worth bragging about because their length and pace would impress no runner. Getting down to the little efforts, you now see, is at least as important as getting up for the big ones.

You promise yourself not to get greedy again anytime soon. That vow will last until you forget how bad your last illness or injury-forced vacation felt. It's best to develop a long memory so you never forget the worst of days. This adds to your appreciation of days that are back to normal.

Lesson 99: Race Spacing

There is life after racing, even though you may not think so in the days and weeks afterward. Once you've thought and talked the race to death, once the euphoria has worn off, the post-race blues are likely to follow. We're not talking about post-race pains. You expect stiffness in the thighs and calves, and you wear your limp like a badge of courage. What you weren't prepared to deal with was the subtle damage—the lingering deadness in your legs, and an even more devastating deadness of spirit. You don't feel like running.

This effect is partly physiological, partly psychological. The goal that pulled you along for weeks or months is gone now, and nothing

After pushing yourself to prepare for a race it might be hard to get back to a regular routine when the race is past—your mind and body both need time to heal.

new has yet replaced it. Some loss of enthusiasm is inevitable. The psyche will heal along with the body, however, if you give them time. This healing takes more time than most runners imagine, and the worst mistake you can make now is to rush that natural timetable.

Racing is like a vaccine. The right dose can make you faster than you've ever been before, but too much of it can hurt. Overracing—racing too often without enough recovery and re-building time in between—is the most common cause of injuries and poor performances.

Two innovative coaches on different sides of the world, Arthur Lydiard of New Zealand and Ernst van Aaken of Germany, hinted at how often a person can race. Lydiard said racing should amount to no more than 10 percent of one's running. Van Aaken went even lower, limiting it to 5 percent of total. Using these formulas, a runner is limited to one racing mile or kilometer in every 10 to 20. And if you take frequent speed or distance tests, the amount of racing should be much less.

One method of insuring that races are spaced properly is to multiply the race distance or time by 10, then not race again until you've put in at least that much easy recovery running. This formula automatically lets you race more often at shorter, less taxing distances and less frequently at longer, tougher ones.

Jack Foster, a New Zealander who ran a 2:11 marathon at age 41 and survived into his 50s as a top-level runner, offered an even simpler rule for clearing away the debris of the race. Foster said he won't allow himself to run hard again until one day has passed for every mile of the race. That's about a week after a 10K, two weeks after a half marathon, and a month after a marathon. One easy day per mile is a good safety margin. One day per kilometer might work even better.

The excitement and effort of racing take a toll, both physically and emotionally. You repay this debt after the race. The longer the event, the longer the recovery period usually needs to be. Allow at least one easy week after the shortest races and one easy day for each mile to kilometer of the longer races. Table 15.1 summarizes these recommendations. A simpler formula is one easy week per hour of racing. Run nothing long or fast early in this period, and race again only after minimum recovery time has passed.

Lesson 100: Numbers Games

You look up at the overhead clock as you cross the finish line. At the same time, you click off the digital watch on your wrist. You compare the two times and accept the faster one. The first thing you must know when a race ends is, "What was my time?" The second is, "What does it mean?"

The first victory is finishing. The second is running a distance faster than you have before, or at least faster than you expected. Time for a distance shows more than what happens here and now.

Table 15.1   Downtime

Race length	Recovery period
5K (3.1 miles)	1 week
8K (5.0 miles)	1 week
10K (6.2 miles)	1 to 2 weeks
12K (7.5 miles)	1 to 2 weeks
15K (9.3 miles)	2 to 3 weeks
20K (12.4 miles)	2 to 3 weeks
Half-marathon (13.1 miles/21.1K)	2 to 3 weeks
25K (15.5 miles)	3 to 4 weeks
30K (18.7 miles)	3 to 5 weeks
20 miles (32.2K)	3 to 5 weeks
Marathon (26.2 miles/42.2K)	4 to 6 weeks

Unlike sports with arbitrary scoring systems—baseball, tennis, golf, and most others—running results cross lines of time and space. Chicago's NBA score against Los Angeles on Sunday tells only what the two teams did against each other that day. It says little about how each might have done against New York, or how well they met their own standards of perfection.

Running times transcend these limits. A miler from Chicago can race against one from Los Angeles today and know how he or she might have done against one from New York racing someplace else. Not only that, but people racing in the year 2000 can compete against marks left behind in 1900. This year's runners can leave records for people to break in 2100.

Best of all, runners can compete against their own histories and be winners without being the first to finish. Time is your most important result. It not only lets you race this distance with these people, it also lets you compare your races with all other races at all distances you have ever or will ever run. This is why you must know your time as you finish. This is why you work out its meanings. It is to complete a page in your history. You have your time. Now start processing it. Get it ready to go into your history book in a form you understand and can compare with earlier and later times.

1. **Compare your time with another known standard**. This race may have been an odd distance, like 11 kilometers (6.8 miles). Your time of 52:36 doesn't tell you much, so reduce it to a minutes-per-mile (or kilometer) pace. Pace per mile carries more meaning than overall time because you judge all running, training, and racing by this standard. You know immediately after making this calculation

Use your post-race running workouts as race recovery.

how much faster you raced than you normally run, or how much farther you were able to hold a pace than you do in everyday runs.

2. **Compare your time with your other times at this distance**. Times gain meaning as you run standard distances again and again— or as you race the same course repeatedly. You set personal records and store them in your diary and memory. You break them or know exactly how far you miss them.

3. **Compare this time with those from other events**. You might enter a 10K race this week, a half-marathon next week, and a 5K a few weeks later. So how do you compare the results from different distances? Start by figuring pace. Then determine a normal slow-down/speedup factor from one distance to another. (Lessons 73, 80, 88, and 94, pages 133, 145, 157, and 167 guide you through this process.) The results show if you're faster or slower than expected. They also predict pace for an unfamiliar distance before you race it.

4. **Compare your projected and actual times for this distance**. (These again come from tables in earlier chapters.) A time considerably slower than predicted indicates you have made training errors. Most likely, either the speed or the distance training was inadequate. On the other hand, a faster-than-expected time is to be celebrated. Not only did you do well in this race, but you probably can expect similar improvement across the board.

5. **Compare your pace for the first and second halves of the race**. A dramatic slowdown in the latter stages indicates an overly aggressive start, probably to the detriment of your overall time. A closing rush much faster than the opening means that you probably lost more time early than you could make up. (See Lessons 82, 83, 89, and 96 on pages 147, 148, 158, and 170 for pacing advice.)

Two more comparisons are optional. These match you against other runners in a race field. Don't think you have lost if you don't match up well here. The real race is with the distance and your own times.

6. **Compare yourself with everyone else who raced with you**. Your overall place is only a beginning. You give that number more meaning by turning it into a percentage ranking. Divide your place by the number of starters. For example, you were 98th of 609. This ranks you in the top 16 percent. In the next race, you might rank 200th of 2,000. The place may be lower, but the rating of 10 percent

is better. This system lets you compare accurately your finishes in different-sized events.

7. **Compare yourself with others of your age group and sex.** In long-distance races everyone usually starts together, but the results are split into divisions to make up for the inequities between young and old, male and female. See how you rank beside runners like yourself, dividing your group place by the number of its starters to get another percentage that compares you with the people most like you.

Lesson 101: Seasonal Variations

A runner can't sow and reap at the same time, which is another way of saying that the time for building up between races must far exceed the time spent tearing down during them. You now know this to be true from race to race, but the principle also applies to seasons of the year. We need to follow each season of heavy racing with an extended period of recovery and rebuilding.

Arthur Lydiard said a racer can hold peak form for three or four months before taking time off from racing. Tom Osler reached the same conclusion independently. He wrote, "One can rarely maintain a high performance level for more than three months."

Osler observed that he passed through cycles lasting about six months, each cycle including one high and one low period roughly corresponding to the seasons of the year. He found that he raced best during the highs and prefers to run casually during the lows.

"The six-month performance cycle is of importance for several reasons," wrote Osler. "For one, it allows you to predict which times of the year you will perform best. Likewise it allows you to determine when you should take a less serious attitude toward racing. Harder, shorter, faster runs can be tolerated during the peak phase and can produce dramatically improved racing performances. Easier, slower, longer training runs are best during the low phase."

Osler's advice grows more important as races spread throughout the year and there no longer is any off-season to the racing schedule. The pattern to adopt is alternating seasons of highs and lows (for instance, high in the spring and autumn to take advantage of the

Take advantage of the different seasons to change the way you run.

best weather; low in the summer and winter when conditions are least attractive for racing). The pattern to avoid is putting two or more serious racing seasons back to back. In the timeless words of Ecclesiastes, everything has its season, "a time to sow and a time to reap, a time to break down and a time to build up."

Running Planner

The programs in this book aren't the only ways to train and race. But they have proved themselves to be good ways to balance short-term success and satisfaction with long-term health and enjoyment. We close out the book by summarizing its content and simplifying your planning, based on advice from the preceding 101 lessons. The tables and tips presented here are aimed mainly at runners who race. Photocopy these pages so you can use them repeatedly.

Your Easy Runs

Plan your schedule of easy runs by determining the following information.

1. How far to train on the recovery runs that should make up the majority of your days (see Lesson 40, page 70)

   Indicate the current average length of your easy runs (in miles or kilometers).

   _____

   Indicate the average pace (per mile or kilometers).

   _____

   Calculate the typical amount of time (in minutes) of your easy runs, multiplying distance by pace.

   _____

If the total time is less than 30 minutes, you need to run more. If it is more than 60 minutes, you should run less on these days. The ideal range for easy runs (not including long or fast races and rehearsals for them) is a half hour to an hour.

Recommended shortest distance on easy runs, dividing 30 minutes by typical pace

_____

Recommended longest distance on easy runs, dividing 60 minutes by typical pace

_____

2. How fast to train; pace should be comfortable, neither too fast nor too slow (see Lesson 41, page 72)

Indicate your most recent short-distance race time (5K to 12K), or estimate current potential.

_____

Calculate your average pace per mile or kilometer, dividing the time by the distance.

_____

That figure represents your current maximum pace for the approximate distance of your daily runs.

Indicate your current average pace for easy runs.

_____

Copy your short-distance race pace from above.

_____

Subtract your race pace from your training pace.

_____

If the difference between maximum and daily pace for this distance is less than one minute per mile (38 seconds per kilometer), you are training too fast. If the gap is more than two minutes per mile (1:15 per kilometer), your training is too slow. Calculate your ideal easy-run pace by adding one to two minutes per mile (38 seconds to 1:15 per kilometer) to your current short-distance race pace.

Recommended fastest training pace on easy days

_____

Recommended slowest training pace on easy days

_____

3. How often to train easily; three days is the minimum and six days the maximum

   Indicate the number of days each week on which you typically run.

   _____

   Indicate the number of hard days (longer or faster than normal, including races).

   _____

   Indicate the number of rest days.

   _____

If the number of easy runs is seven, schedule one day of rest and possibly one hard day. If the number of easy runs is three or fewer, boost it to four or five a week.

Your Rehearsing

Plan your pre-race rehearsals (which are tests under racelike conditions of speed or distance) by determining the following information.

1. Basic training, which is the sum of all the running you have done recently

    Indicate the average length of your runs from the past month (in minutes).

    _____

    If you have averaged less than 30 minutes, racing is not recommended. Delay entering any events or attempting any racelike rehearsals until you have increased your daily average to a half hour or more. If you have averaged more than 30 minutes, your training has prepared you for the rehearsals recommended in this book. Maintain an average of at least a half hour per day. You are preparing to test yourself at about twice the length of your typical training run, unless a longer limit is indicated in section 2, below.

    Indicate the average pace of your easy runs from the past month (per mile or kilometer).

    _____

    You are prepared for race rehearsals at a pace up to two minutes per mile (1:15 per kilometer) faster than you typically train, unless a faster limit is indicated in section 3.

    _____

2. Distance limit, which is as far as you can now safely run
   Indicate the length of your longest run within the past month
   (in hours and minutes).

   _____

   This amount represents the longest time you are currently
   prepared to race. To extend that limit, follow the distance-
   extending recommendations in Lessons 68, 86, and 93, pages
   121, 153, and 166.

3. Speed limit, which is as fast as you can now safely run
   Indicate the pace of your fastest run within the past month
   (per mile or kilometer).

   _____

   This figure represents the fastest pace you are currently prepared to race. To extend that limit, follow the speed-improv-
   ing recommendations in Lessons 57, 77, and 78, pages 100,
   140, and 141.

Your Racing

Plan your racing potential and pace by determining the following
information.

1. Race description for your next event
   Indicate the race distance in kilometers or miles.

   _____

   Indicate your time goal for this race.

   _____

Calculate the pace required to achieve this goal (per mile or kilometer, dividing time by distance).

_____

Indicate the average length of your daily runs during the past month (in minutes).

_____

Calculate the difference in length between this race and the average runs (time longer or shorter).

_____

Indicate your longest race or rehearsal within the past month (in hours and minutes).

_____

Calculate the difference in length between this race and the longest recent race or rehearsal (time longer or shorter).

_____

Indicate the average pace (per mile or kilometer) of your easy runs during the past month.

_____

Calculate the difference in pace between this race and your average easy-run pace (time faster or slower).

_____

Indicate your fastest race or rehearsal within the past month (pace per mile or kilometer).

_____

Calculate the difference in pace between this race and the fastest recent race or rehearsal (time faster or slower).

_____

You should have rehearsed at least once at or near the full time of the race (but at a slower pace), and at least once at or near the race's full pace (but at a shorter distance).

2. Personal record for this racing distance
   Indicate the best time you have run in this event.

_____

Calculate the pace for your record time (per mile or kilometer, dividing time by distance).

_____

Indicate your target pace in the current race (from section 1, above).

_____

Calculate the difference between your target pace and your record pace (faster or slower).

_____

3. Time projection, or how fast you can realistically expect to run in the upcoming race

List your most recent race distance.

_____

List your final time in that race.

_____

List your pace per mile or kilometer in that race.

_____

If you are racing again at the same distance after no major changes in training, and if the weather and course conditions are similar, the times in the last race and this one should be comparable. If you are racing at a different distance, refer to Lessons 73, 80, 88, and 94 (pages 133, 145, 157, and 167) for comparable times.

Indicate your projected race time (based on the appropriate table).

_____

Calculate your projected race pace (per mile or kilometer, dividing time by distance).

_____

Actual race time probably will fall somewhere between your goal (in section 1, above) and the projection from the table. Select a realistic figure as a basis for outlining a pacing plan.

4. Pacing advice, for running up to your capabilities and within your limits. The most important checkpoint in any race lies at or near halfway. Calculate your ideal time at that point.

Halfway distance (divide length of race by two)

_____

Half of total projected time (from section 3)

_____

Average pace to achieve the projected time (from section 3)

_____

Fastest starting pace (subtract five seconds per mile from average pace, or three per kilometer)

_____

Fastest halfway time (multiply maximum starting pace by halfway distance)

_____

Slowest starting pace (add five seconds per mile to average pace, or three seconds per kilometer)

_____

Slowest halfway time (multiply minimum starting pace by halfway distance)

_____

Lessons 82, 83, 89, and 96 (pages 147, 148, 158, and 170) give recommended paces for the most popular racing distances—5K, 10K, half marathon, and marathon.

Your Review

Review your race and plan for future racing by determining the following information.

1. Time analysis, or how your splits added up
   Indicate your race distance (in kilometers or miles).

   _____

   Indicate your final race time.

   _____

   Calculate your race pace (per mile or kilometer, dividing time by distance).

   _____

   Indicate your previous best time (personal record) at this distance.

   _____

   Compare the result from this race with your previous best (time faster or slower).

   _____

2. Projection analysis, or how close you came to the predicted time

Indicate your projected time for this race.

_____

Calculate the amount by which you missed the projection (faster or slower).

_____

A faster-than-expected time indicates that you underestimated your potential; aim higher in the next race. It also suggests that your times at other distances (those on which the prediction was based) are due for improvement. A time slower than the projection generally means that you have trained inadequately, paced yourself improperly, or both. Make the necessary corrections before and during your next race.

3. Pace analysis, or how evenly you spread your efforts over the full distance

Indicate your time for the first half of the race (estimate if necessary, based on nearby splits).

_____

Indicate the distance of the first half (in kilometers or miles).

_____

Calculate your pace in the first half (per mile or kilometer, dividing time by distance).

_____

Calculate your time for the second half (subtract time for first half from total time).

_____

Calculate your pace in the second half.

_____

Calculate the difference in pace between first half and second half (subtract lower from higher figure).

_____

4. Place analysis, or how well you did against other runners. Indicate your placing in this race (estimating if necessary).

Overall placing

_____

Total number of starters

_____

Placing among men or women

_____

Number of men or women

_____

Placing in your age group

_____

Number in this age group

_____

A percentage ranking gives a realistic picture of how you placed in comparison to other runners in races and divisions of varying sizes. Calculate those percentages.

Overall finish (divide your place by total number of starters)

_____

Female or male finish (divide your place in this category by its number of starters)

_____

Age-group finish (divide your place in this category by its number of starters)

_____

5. Recovery advice, or how long before you should run hard again (see Lesson 99 on page 176)

   Indicate the distance of the race (kilometers or miles).

_____

   Calculate your recommended number of recovery days (one easy or rest day for each kilometer or 1-1/2 days per mile of the race).

_____

Determine your minimum recovery period in weeks (divide number of days above by seven, then round up to the next higher full week).

Avoid further races or rehearsals until this number of weeks have passed, but continue easy runs during this period. Additional recovery guidelines: (1) rest one day immediately afterward for each hour of the race; (2) don't allow the amount of racing or race rehearsing in any month to exceed 10 percent of total running time.

Index

About the Author

Joe Henderson combined his passion for running with his natural talent for writing and became one of the most prolific running writers on the planet. Although Henderson never accomplished his first career goal of becoming a high school or college running coach, through his advice in hundreds of magazines and books and in frequent speeches to running groups, he has indirectly coached thousands of runners.

Henderson was born in Illinois in 1943 and grew up in Iowa, where he began running at age 14. After graduating from Drake University, he began his work in running journalism at *Track & Field News*. Today he continues as a columnist with *Runner's World* and as the publisher of the newsletter *Running Commentary*. He has authored and coauthored 22 books including the best-selling *Marathon Training* as well as four others from Human Kinetics—*Best Runs, Better Runs, Coaching Cross Country Successfully,* and *Fitness Running*.

Henderson has twice been named Journalist of the Year by the Road Runners Club of America. He is also a member of the Club's Hall of Fame. Henderson now lives in Eugene, Oregon, with his wife, Barbara Shaw.

Books by Joe Henderson

Long, Slow Distance

Road Racers and Their Training

Thoughts on the Run

Run Gently, Run Long

The Long Run Solution

Jog, Run, Race

Run Farther, Run Faster

The Running Revolution

Running, A to Z

Running Your Best Race

Running for Fitness, for Sport and for Life

Joe Henderson's Running Handbook

Total Fitness

Think Fast

Masters Running and Racing (with Bill Rodgers and Priscilla Welch)

Fitness Running (with Richard Brown)

Did I Win?

Better Runs

Road Racers and Their Training

Marathon Training

Best Runs

Run your *best* yet

Better Runs is both an inspirational and instructional book that will boost your motivation, performance, and enjoyment as a runner. The book is filled with anecdotes and insights on training, racing, and much, much more.

Better Runs is full of time-tested advice on how to

- be a winner in running, regardless of your ability and ambition;
- balance your training by rotating workout distances;
- measure, record, and analyze your times and distances;
- improve racing with more efficient pacing;
- supplement running with other exercises;
- set challenging yet reachable running goals;
- establish good eating habits; and
- prevent injuries and treat your own ailments.

264 pp • ISBN 0-87322-866-9
$15.95 ($22.95 Canadian)

Best Runs contains more than 100 essays that will inform, inspire, and amuse all readers, from fitness runners to hardcore competitors. Each of the book's 25 chapters serves as a valuable lesson in running. You'll find entertaining tales and proven advice on how to

- reduce the time pressures associated with training and racing;
- decrease down-time by listening to your heart and early warning signals;
- follow an optimal running diet;
- reduce your anxiety before races;
- improve long distance running techniques;
- enjoy running into your later years; and
- much, much more.

256 pp •ISBN 0-88011-896-2
$15.95 ($22.95 Canadian)